A · M · P · L · E
MANSIONS

A M P L E
MANSIONS

The Viceregal Residences of the Canadian Provinces

UNIVERSITY OF OTTAWA PRESS
Ottawa • London • Paris

R.H. HUBBARD

© University of Ottawa Press, 1989

ISBN 0-7766-0277-2

Canadian Cataloguing in Publication Data

Hubbard, R. H. (Robert Hamilton), 1916–
    Ample mansions: the viceregal residences of the Canadian
    provinces

Includes bibliographical references.
ISBN 0-7766-0277-2

1. Governors—Canada—Dwellings.
2. Lieutenant-governors—Canada—Dwellings.
3. Historic buildings—Canada. I. Title.

NA4445.C3H92 1989   971   C86-090282-X

Book and jacket design by Anita Bergmann and Jan Soetermans
Printed in Canada
by Tri-Graphic Printing (Ottawa) Limited

The Publishers acknowledge, with gratitude, the financial
assistance of the Jules and Gabrielle Léger Fellowship Fund of
the Social Sciences and Humanities Research Council, and of the
Canada Council in the production of this book.

For Their Honours
The Lieutenant Governors of the Provinces

C O N T E N T S

F O R E W O R D

If any justification were needed for me to write a preface to this book, it would be close at hand in Dr Hubbard's book of 1977, *Rideau Hall, An Illustrated History of Government House, Ottawa*. Two of my distinguished predecessors saw fit to write prefaces to it: General Georges P. Vanier to Part One (which he commissioned as a centennial project in 1967) and Jules Léger who inspired the writing of Part Two. Incidentally, it is my hope that this book, now more than a decade old, may soon be brought up to date and supplemented with an account of the Governor General's residence in the Citadel, Quebec.

The present volume forms a natural complement to the earlier one on Rideau Hall. Dealing with the past and present residences of the governors and lieutenant governors of all our provinces, it thus includes the houses inhabited by the governors of New France and British North America, as well as those of Ontario and the Atlantic and western provinces. More than that, it brings to our attention for the first time not only architectural monuments neglected by historians, but also the roles of those who over the years have exercised the headship of state in the name of the Sovereign in the various parts of our land and provided visible centres for community pride.

I am well aware of the painstaking research, and of the many visits to the existing houses, which have enabled the author to write with authority on these houses and their inhabitants. In the expectation of still further fruits of his labours I welcome this latest contribution to our knowledge of history and art and commend it to a wide readership.

Jeanne Sauvé

*T*his is a history of the official residences of the governors and lieutenant governors of all the provinces of present-day Canada. Over a period of two centuries the usual name for such buildings, not only in Canada but in other parts of the British Empire, was Government House. The fact that the name has no exact equivalent in other languages besides English is an indication of its origin and evolution.

Though the *Oxford English Dictionary* dates it from India in 1845, the term was in use in the Old Empire well before the American Revolution, apparently at first more as a generic than a proper name. Of necessity the government of any new overseas possession was centred in a single building which housed both the governor's lodgings and his offices. This building was indeed the "government" house of the colony.

By the middle of the eighteenth century the senior colonies had provided themselves with separate houses for their Assemblies and administrative offices. Such buildings received the name of State or Province House — and in Williamsburg, capital of that grandest of American provinces, the Neo-Classic one of Capitol. In Williamsburg too the governor's house was called the Palace; but in other places (along with "Governor's Mansion"*) the older name of Government House was retained. In the nineteenth-century Empire, so uniform was the use of Government House that in the 1880s Queen Victoria saw fit to rebuke Lady Stanley, wife of the Governor General of Canada, for dating her letters from Rideau Hall, the name given to her Ottawa house by its original private owner.[1]

In Canada the earliest use of "Government House" dates from the late eighteenth century, with reference to the residence being prepared for Halifax.

In a number of American state capitals today there are "Executive Mansions".

Subsequent uses were at Fredericton in 1816, St John's in 1825 and Charlottetown in 1832. Quebec was the exception. The old name of the Château Saint-Louis survived the Cession of 1760; and that of its successor Spencer Wood was retained for a century after the purchase of that house in 1852 as a residence for Lord Elgin. In the other provinces "Government House" was the rule, though at Victoria the apt nickname of Cary Castle clung to a house bought by the governor in 1865, and in Toronto the fourth and last Government House was most generally known as Chorley Park after the property on which it was built. In the federal capital "Rideau Hall" has continued to alternate with "Government House" in spite of Queen Victoria's stricture. Only in recent years has an attempt been made to resolve not only the problem of two names for the one house but also that of two official languages — by heading the note-paper "Rideau Hall" and adding "Government House" and "Résidence du Gouverneur général" as sub-headings — just in case anyone should be left in doubt.

❧

This book does not attempt to be a constitutional or political history of governors and lieutenant governors of the provinces, that field having been admirably covered by Professor Saywell.[2] Yet some little background is needed for an understanding of these officials and their houses. As Jacques Monet has noted, the office of Governor General is the one institution which has enjoyed an uninterrupted existence from the beginnings of our history to the present day,[3] by the substitution of a George for a Louis in 1760. This statement also applies by extension to the office of governor or lieutenant governor in each province. In each of the other provinces besides Canada which made up British North America before 1867 a governor or lieutenant governor, technically subject to the governor general in Quebec but in practice responsible to the Colonial Office in London, was present from the beginning. Newfoundland had a long line of summer naval governors before the permanent settlement of the country had reached a stage where a resident civil governor was required.

After Confederation the responsibility of the lieutenant governors of provinces was transferred from London to Ottawa. At the outset they exercised powers of disallowance and reservation of provincial legislation on behalf of the central government, but the practice gradually lapsed and court action took its place. In addition, since the Statute of Westminster, just as the Governor General ceased to represent the British government and became solely the Sovereign's representative, so lieutenant governors have tended to act as royal representatives in their provinces.

But the continuing appointment of lieutenant governors by the Governor General in Council, i.e. the party in power in Ottawa, leaves the door open to dispute. It has in some cases led provincial political leaders, after lost battles with the central authority, to vent their wrath on their lieutenant governors. Powerless to abolish the office, several provinces have closed the houses they had maintained as official residences. Thus in 1937, Ontario's squabble with the Mackenzie King administration, and Alberta's with the same authority in 1938, resulted in the abandonment of two fine houses. But long before this, in 1893, economic conditions in New Brunswick had brought about the closing of a great house in Fredericton. In 1945 a depressed economy and the populism of the government in power in Saskatchewan were involved in the closing of Government House in Regina.

Yet the majority of the provinces today — all except Ontario and Saskatchewan — maintain official residences. The recent constitutional deliberations, which have left the Monarchy intact, may indeed reflect a revival of respect for the place of the Crown.

Most of the older Government Houses still exist, and of these nearly all have been inhabited continuously or nearly so by their rightful occupants. Of those which have been closed, only the house in Toronto is gone forever. The Regina house has been restored as a museum, but the lieutenant governor has very recently moved at least his offices into it after a long exile. Yet another, in Edmonton, has become a conference centre, but a smaller house has been bought for the lieutenant governor. Old Government House in Fredericton having long been a regional headquarters for the Mounted Police, a smaller house has been provided pending restoration. The present house in Quebec, replacing the lost Bois-de-Coulonge, has survived a recent threat of closure; but there, as in Toronto, spacious official quarters for the lieutenant governor exist in government buildings.

All provinces today feel the need of a place for official entertaining, and this they provide in one form or another. But those with no active Government House lack any accommodation for visiting heads of state, to say nothing of the Queen and other members of the Royal Family, whose visits have become more and more frequent.

In view of the fact that Government Houses have always been centres of the official and social life of their provinces, it is curious that published material on them is so scarce. It is limited to a few monographs, occasional references in diaries, and brief descriptions by historians in setting the scene for political events. It was to remedy this situation that I visited all the provincial capitals with the intention of writing a short architectural and social history of all houses past and present along with accounts of their more colourful occupants and events — and all this in order to provide a complement to my book on Rideau Hall. [4]

My further purpose has been to awaken an interest in, and appreciation of, an important part of our heritage, so that existing houses may be maintained, the abandoned restored and the lost rebuilt, and that the contributions of their occupants should not be forgotten.

My work has been largely done at Rideau Hall. The encouragement I received there from the late General Georges P. Vanier, and from his two immediate successors, resulted in the Rideau Hall book. It also led me on to the present topic, which I broached in 1977 in a paper read to the Royal Society of Canada.[5] The detailed research necessary to expand this work was made possible by the awarding to me of the Jules and Gabrielle Léger Fellowship for 1981; and I am much indebted to the officers of the Social Sciences and Humanities Research Council, who administer the Fellowship, for assistance in the publication of this book. A particular debt is owed to the Right Honourable Edward R. Schreyer and Her Excellency Jeanne Sauvé who, after my retirement as Cultural Adviser to the Governor General, have allowed me space in Rideau Hall in which to continue my work. I also offer thanks to Mr Esmond Butler, former Secretary to the Governor General, for his unfailing support of my studies over many years. I am also grateful to the Ontario Arts Council for a grant which has helped with the illustrations.

No less important have been the assistance and hospitality extended to me by past and present lieutenant governors of the provinces and their respective secretaries. They have warmly received me into their houses so that I could study the architecture at first hand and savour the life that went on inside them. My admiration has grown considerably for the devotion and energy with which they carry out their responsibilities. I warmly acknowledge the help so kindly extended to me, especially in the matter of illustrations, by the Royal Archives, Windsor Castle. The public archives of all the provinces have been major sources of documents and illustrations, and my thanks go to their capable and helpful staffs.

R.H.H.
Rideau Hall
1989

New France

Beginnings in Acadia
Quebec 1608-1759
Louisbourg

6

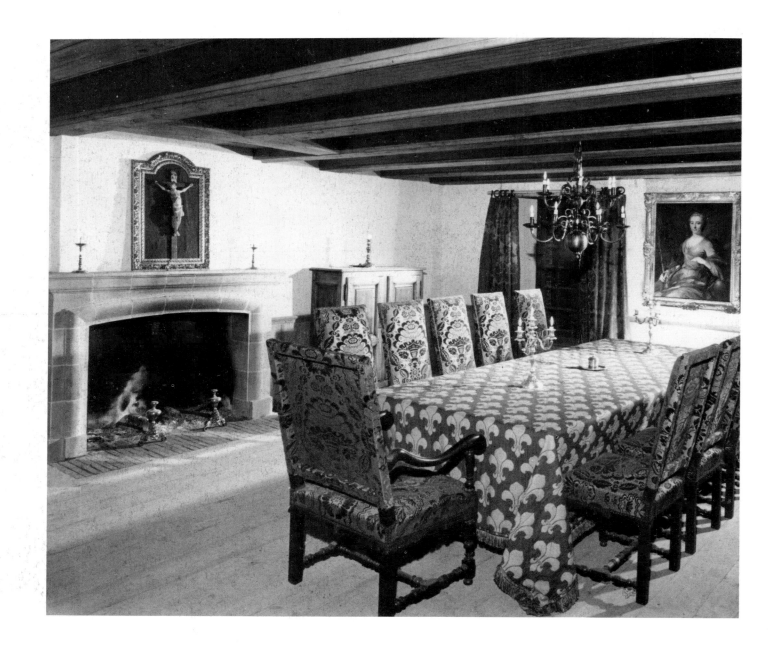

The Council Room, Château of Louisbourg, reconstructed.

Beginnings in Acadia

By one of history's minor quirks the site of the first dwelling of a royal representative in French Canada is now in the United States. The tiny Île Sainte-Croix, now called Dochet Island, lies in the middle of the St Croix River, which bounds the province of New Brunswick on the west. The international boundary, drawn in the last years of the eighteenth century, placed it in the state of Maine.

In 1603 the French Calvinist explorer Pierre Du Gua de Monts became head of a company to which Henri IV granted privileges of trade and settlement in "Acadia, Canada and other places in New France". De Monts bore the title of Lieutenant General to the King. In June 1604 he arrived in Passamaquoddy Bay and chose the little island as an outpost secure from attack. Accompanying him was the versatile explorer Samuel de Champlain as geographer and cartographer to the expedition. The company also included Jean de Bien-court de Poutrincourt as senior officer, the trader François Gravé du Pont, two surgeons, a chaplain and a company of artisans.

The "habitation" which they built took the form of a dozen or so small timber houses grouped on a rectangular plot and connected in some places by a palisade. Besides living quarters for de Monts, Champlain and the other gentlemen there were dormitories for the soldiers and artisans, a chapel, a community house, a mill, a blacksmith's shop and a kitchen. Excavations carried out in modern times indicate that the schematic plan which Champlain published in his *Voyages* is roughly accurate. Also revealed were the graves of those, nearly half the company, who died of scurvy during the terrible winter of 1604-5, which made of the island a pestilential prison. Frozen cider doled out by the pound failed to arrest the disease.[1]

This experience persuaded de Monts to move his settlement to a snug harbour on the north shore of the Annapolis basin. And so in the summer of 1605 the huts were taken apart and the timbers transported by ship for use in building a new habitation at Port-Royal.[2] As illustrated in the *Voyages* it was a more compact arrangement than its predecessor, the houses forming a closed quadrangle. Included were storehouses for supplies and articles of trade, a blacksmith's shop, a chapel, quarters for the officers and men, gardens, a graveyard, bakehouse, kitchen and a gun emplacement. One of the better houses was shared by Champlain and Gravé du Pont. As for de Monts, he departed for France, leaving Champlain to carry out explorations during the temperate months of the year.

The winter months once more brought scurvy, but the mild winter of 1606-7 was more pleasantly spent. To raise the men's spirits Champlain invented the "Order of Good Cheer" in which a ruler of the feast for each day, adorned with collar and wand, marched round the table with the trophies of the hunt. A good deal of wine was consumed.

After Théophile Hamel: Samuel de Champlain. Lithograph.

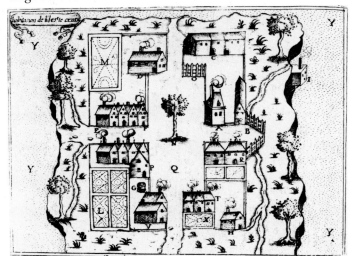

After Samuel de Champlain: Habitation de l'île Ste Croix. *Woodcut in the* Voyages *of 1613.*

Champlain's Habitation at Port-Royal, near Lower Granville, Nova Scotia, reconstructed 1939.

Accompanying Poutrincourt when he rejoined the expedition in 1606 was Marc Lescarbot, a Paris lawyer, traveller and writer. And when, later in that same year, Poutrincourt and Champlain returned from their perilous travels along the coast, they were greeted by a masque, *Théâtre de Neptune*. It had been written by Lescarbot and was performed in boats in the harbour by Frenchmen and Indians. It was the first theatrical presentation in North America. In 1939, on the basis of Champlain's description of the habitation at Port-Royal, the Canadian government reconstructed the buildings on the original site near Lower Granville, Nova Scotia.

The monopoly granted to de Monts expired in 1607, and the expedition returned to France. Acadia was revived when Poutrincourt returned in 1610, but in his temporary absence from Port-Royal, Argall's raiders from Jamestown destroyed the fort — which was partially restored by Poutrincourt's son Charles de Biencourt in 1615. Sir William Alexander, during the abortive attempt of 1629 to found a Scottish colony, built a new fort. Acadia, the little settlement which grew out of Port-Royal after its restitution to France in 1632, then proceeded on its turbulent history, somehow surviving the frequent changes of hands between the French and English, to say nothing of the struggle for power among its own administrators. In the 1630s the fort was rebuilt on the south shore of the Annapolis Basin, but presumably little was left of it when by the Peace of Breda the English handed Acadia back to the French in 1667. In any case the governor lived for a time at Pentagoet (now Castine, Maine) on the Penobscot River.

Another restoration of the fort was undertaken by Louis de Meneval in 1689, but he was obliged to surrender it to Sir William Phips the following year. Rebuilding was resumed under Mombeton de Brouillan; and a powder magazine built by Daniel d'Auger de Subercase in 1708 survives today in Fort Anne Historic Park. But Port-Royal was once again captured, this time in 1710 by the New Englanders under Francis Nicholson, who renamed it Annapolis Royal; and in 1713 the Nova Scotia mainland was finally ceded to Britain, with only Île Royale (Cape Breton) remaining in French hands. The rivalry between the two colonial powers was then resumed on a greater scale, with the British installed at Annapolis Royal and the French at Louisbourg.

Abitasion du port royal

After Samuel de Champlain:
Abitasion du port royal. *Woodcut in*
the Voyages *of 1613.*

Quebec 1608-1759

Meanwhile, in the spring of 1608, Champlain had sailed up the St Lawrence and after stopping at Tadoussac had fixed upon the point of Quebec[3] for his post, evidently recognizing its grandeur and natural strategic importance. Now designated lieutenant to de Monts, he built a habitation similar to that of Port-Royal. It stood close to the river's edge on a site now occupied by the Place Royal and the church of Notre-Dame-des-Victoires. His representation of it in the *Voyages*[4] shows three substantial blocks of wooden houses with large chimneys. The plan was like that of Port-Royal, if less regular because of gun platforms angled into the St Lawrence. As Champlain himself reported at the end of the first summer,

> I continued the construction of our quarters, which contained three main buildings of three stories . . . . Each one was three fathoms long and two and a half wide. The storehouse was six long and three wide, with a fine cellar six feet high. All the way round our buildings I had a gallery made, outside the second storey, which was a very convenient thing. There were also ditches fifteen feet wide and six deep, and outside these I made several salients which enclosed a part of the buildings, and there we put our cannon. In front of the building there is an open space four fathoms wide and six or seven long, which abuts upon the river's bank. Round about the buildings are very good gardens.[5]

The buildings, arranged in an open quadrangle, constituted a fort. Visible in Champlain's illustration are a sundial, a dovecote to ensure a fresh supply of meat in winter, and buildings designated as stores, workers' lodgings, forge and kitchen, besides quarters for the officers and men. Champlain's own quarters were fairly substantial, occupying the ground floor of one of the larger blocks.

After Samuel de Champlain: Abitation de Qvebecq. *Woodcut in the* Voyages *of 1613.*

The early months of 1609 brought intense cold and the dread scurvy which spared only eight of the company of twenty-eight. In December 1610, after two seasons of exploration and of conflict with the Iroquois, he was in Paris to marry his young bride Hélène Boullé but returned alone to Quebec in 1611. On another visit to Paris the following year he was given the powers of a governor without title of commission.

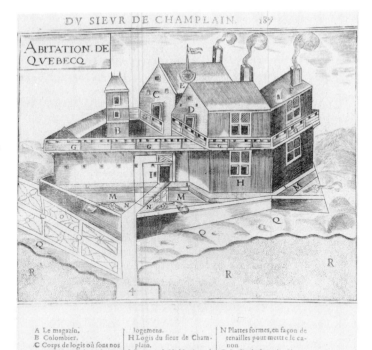

planned to improve the compound by adding a new building inside the walls. Construction began in May 1624, three months before their return to France. When Champlain returned to Quebec alone in 1626 he found the building still incomplete. When it was finished, it had at the ends of one of its walls twin turrets, the stone foundations of which have come to light in recent excavations of the Place Royale. Later in the seventeenth century the building was used as a King's warehouse; but it was in a ruinous condition by the time it was destroyed in the Lower Town fire of 1682.[6]

Meanwhile, in 1620, a more significant structure had risen on the cliff above the town, commanding the narrows of the St Lawrence. It stood on a site that was to be occupied by governors for more than two centuries. Within the palisade of this Fort Saint-Louis was built the first "château" of Quebec — a house which, having lost its roof in a storm, received a replacement in 1626. At this same time the fort was also rebuilt with earthworks. It was this stronghold which Champlain was obliged in 1629 to yield to the invading Kirke brothers. Carried off to England, he found his way to France and was appointed lieutenant to Cardinal Richelieu, founder of the Compagnie des Cent Associés. In 1633, a year after the Treaty of Saint-Germain-en-Laye had restored Quebec to the French, Champlain returned to Quebec for the last time. Alone in the château in his old age, he led a devout life, praying in the chapel and hearing devotional readings during his meals. Death came on Christmas Day 1635.

Little is known of the second château on the cliff except for an outline plan drawn in 1634 by his engineer Jean Bourdon (c.1601-1688).[7] Much more is known of the third, which was the first actually to be named Château Saint-Louis. Charles de Montmagny, a member of the Order of Malta who had fought the Turks in the Mediterranean, arrived in 1636 as the first

Jean-Baptiste Louis Franquelin: The Château Saint-Louis, Quebec, of 1647-8, detail from Carte du Fort St. Louis, 1688.

11

In 1620, after a further eight years of exploration, and several visits to France, he brought Hélène to Canada. What the sufferings of this Paris girl were, in a house which had not only deteriorated in the interval but was exposed to attack by Indians and wild animals, are not on record. But on their arrival Champlain

12

titular governor of New France to find his capital pitifully open to attack. In 1647-8, near the end of his term, he demolished Champlain's fort and house and replaced them with stone buildings.

The new Château was considerably larger than the old, though still of one storey. A characteristically French hipped roof (*pavillon*) with dormers covered its long squat bulk. Drawings of it made in 1683 and 1688 by Jean-Baptiste-Louis Franquelin (c.1651-after 1712), and in 1685 by Robert de Villeneuve (c.1645-after 1692)[8] show a platform overhanging the cliff and affording a magnificent view of the river and distant hills. The great buttresses which supported this terrace have survived into our own times, hidden beneath the present-day Dufferin Terrace. Montmagny also planted a garden beside the Château.

The interior[9] of the new house was one room deep; in the absence of a longitudinal corridor, the rooms opened into one another. There was a *salle*, an antechamber, two bedrooms, a *cabinet*, a small servants' hall (or *office* which was the original kitchen) and a larder. A proper kitchen was added to the end of the house in 1678.

In this house, until his departure for France, Montmagny lived as austere a life as had Champlain. Relief from this régime came only at his New Year's levée, one of the earliest on record. On 1 January 1646, as the Jesuits relate, "The soldiers went to salute the governor with their guns; the inhabitants presented their compliments in a body".[10] Montmagny evidently had visions of establishing a wilderness priory of his Order, for he had a stone carved with the cross of Malta and the date 1647. Buried over the years, it turned up during the levelling of the Château courtyard in 1784 and was set into the door jamb of the Château Haldimand, and is now to be seen in a wall near the entrance to the Château Frontenac hotel.

Montmagny's successor as governor was the military engineer Louis d'Ailleboust de Coulonge, who had already settled his family at Montreal. More enterprising than his predecessor, he invited the Indians to a parley at the Château, during which the terrace chose to collapse. When his term ended in 1651 he moved to his fief of Coulonge, at a league's distance to the west of Quebec, where he built a house. Its site was to have future significance for governors of Canada.

Successive governors of the seventeenth century — Jean de Lauson, Pierre d'Argenson and Pierre Davaugour — occupied the Château Saint-Louis without making serious complaint. In 1662, during Davaugour's period, Pope Alexander VII despatched holy relics to Quebec, and on their arrival they were accompanied to the Château by a procession of forty-seven clerics.[11] The following year an earthquake rocked the city, but with what results to the residence we do not know.

The great turning-point in the colony's life came that same year, 1663, when New France reverted from the Company to the Crown and henceforth its government came directly under the king. Its administration resembled that of a province of France and reflected the absolutism of Louis XIV. Three officials held the reins of power: the governor (Augustin de Mézy from 1663 to 1665 and Daniel de Courcelle from 1665 to 1672), the intendant (Jean Talon from 1665 to 1668 and 1670 to 1672) and the bishop (François de Laval, succeeded in 1668 by Jean-Baptiste de Saint-Vallier). By 1665 the population of the capital had hardly attained five hundred. But when in that year the Marquis de Tracy made his grand entry as commander of the forces, a new era of defence and colonization began.

It was not, however, until 1672 that a governor of New France set out deliberately to reflect the effulgence of the Sun King. Soon after his arrival in Quebec, Count Frontenac, a member of the minor nobility, began to plan a capital and residence worthy of the overseas empire of the Crown of France. Finding Montmagny's château in a "pitiful" state, he determined on a proper replacement. But he lived in the old house until his recall in 1682 over his constant wrangling with the other members of the triumvirate. His successors, Joseph de La Barre and the Marquis de Denonville, did little to improve matters before Frontenac rehabilitated himself and returned in 1689. Having stood fast in the fort in 1690 against the invading force of Sir William Phips, he was in a strong enough position to fulfil his ambitions. Two years later he had his military architect François de Lajoüe (c.1656-c.1719) design a new château.[12]

The water-colour views made by Charles de Fonville (1675-1703) in 1699, and by Gédéon de Catalogne (1662-1729) in 1709,[13] show the result. The new house was a much larger stone structure. Its projecting central block was intended to be flanked by lateral pavilions on the courtyard front, of which only one on the north was built at the time; and a string-course separated the two storeys. Construction had got under way in 1694 under the supervision of the mason-contractor Hilaire Bernard de La Rivière, but the work was still unfinished at Frontenac's death in 1698 and was suspended by royal decree in 1700.

In spite of Frontenac this fourth and last Château Saint-Louis exhibited but little of the grandeur of French architecture in the seventeenth century. It was devoid of ornament. With its steep pavilion roofs and plain doorway, and with its severity and simplicity, it resembled more closely the smaller and earlier châteaux of rural France. The most that can be said is that, seen from a distance, it had something of the monumentality of French design.

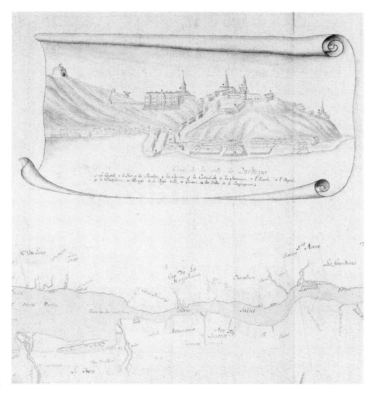

After Charles de Fonville: View of Quebec with the Château Saint-Louis, cartellino on a map of c.1699.

The rooms indoors had low ceilings with exposed beams. On the ground floor were the public rooms and offices, and on the first floor the chapel, bedrooms, dressing rooms, the governor's study and storerooms.

A description by the historian Claude-Charles de La Potherie, who visited Canada between 1698 and 1701, completes the picture:

> The château is on the edge of a great rocky hill twenty *toises* (190 feet) high. Its fortifications are irregular in plan, having two bastions on the side facing the town but no moat. The Governor General's house is 120 feet

Gaspard Chaussegros de Léry: Plans and Elevations for the Château Saint-Louis, Quebec. Drawing, 1724.

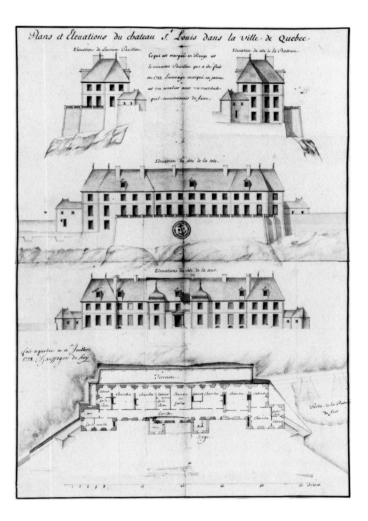

back. It has two storeys but still lacks a wing thirty-three feet long.[14]

Frontenac peopled his house with a considerable staff. These included a chaplain, a doctor, several secretaries, a *corps de garde* and a large number of servants who were well employed in his busy round of dinners, receptions and levées. His amateur theatricals instituted what was to become a tradition in the Government Houses of Canada; but at the time the clergy were scandalized when women were given parts in the plays. More than scandalized was Bishop Saint-Vallier, who excommunicated a young lieutenant who was to have taken the leading part in Molière's *Tartuffe,* a satire on hypocritical clergy, even stooping to bribe the Governor to forbid its performance.

Though New France's population by the time of Frontenac's death in 1698 had increased to twelve thousand or more, and the capital's to two thousand, the Château remained unfinished throughout the period of his successor Louis de Callière. Not until 1719, in the regime of the elder Marquis de Vaudreuil, was the work resumed. Though by that time, in France, the architecture of the Régence had embraced the playful forms of the rococo, the design of 1724 for the completion of the Château, drawn up by the engineer-architect Gaspard Chaussegros de Léry (1682-1756),[15] in no way referred to the newer elements of style, except for a pair of helmeted turrets flanking the entrance and a modest portal with pilasters and pediment. The rest was as plain as ever. Chaussegros, who on the strength of instructions from Paris had vetoed the wilder fancies of the Marquise de Vaudreuil as to interior decoration, had already (1722-3) been obliged to depart from the symmetry of the original scheme, in order to allow more space for the governor's offices, by lengthening the south wing by an extra bay. To restore symmetry, or the illusion of it, he cleverly placed the turrets and vestibule in such a way as to

long, and in front of it an eighty-foot terrace affording a view of the lower town and the waterway. This building is most pleasant, both indoors and out, because of the wings that form its ends at front and mask the extra bay.[16] Unfortunately only the south turret was ever built.

In the enlarged Château, Philippe de Rigaud de Vaudreuil, governor from 1703 to 1725, assumed an importance commensurate with that of Frontenac. He carried out a far-sighted and pro-Canadian policy for the St Lawrence colony and developed a plan for a vast

empire in the interior of the continent. On the domestic scene, his wife in 1710 gave shelter to a little New England girl who had been captured by the Abenaki on one of their raids on the frontier of the English colonies. She grew up to become Mère Esther Wheelwright, the efficient and compassionate superior of the Ursuline Convent in Quebec at the time of the Conquest.

Vaudreuil's successor, the Marquis de Beauharnois, kept a considerable library in the Château, which included the classics, history, literature, geography, architecture, military science and commerce.[17] The Marquis de La Galissonnière, who followed him in 1747, was an authority on the natural history of Canada. It was at the end of his period, in 1749, that the Swedish naturalist Pehr Kalm[18] arrived in Quebec. Armed with a letter of introduction, he met the Governor — "of low stature, and somewhat hump-backed, but of a very agreeable countenance" — and praised him as a new Linnaeus. Kalm's account of Quebec and of his experiences there is couched in the dry and factual style of the scientist:

The *Palace* is situated on the south or steepest side of the mountain, just above the lower city. It is not properly a palace but a large building of stone, two stories high, extending north and south. On the west side of it is a courtyard, surrounded partly by a wall and partly by houses. On the east side, or towards the river, is a gallery as long as the whole building, and about two fathoms broad, paved with smooth flags and protected on the outside by iron railings from which the city and the river exhibit a charming view. This gallery serves as a very agreeable walk after dinner, and those who come to speak with the governor-general wait here till he is at leisure. The palace is the lodging of the governor-general of Canada, and a number of soldiers stand before it, both at the gate and in the courtyard. When the governor or the bishop comes in

After Granicourt: Marquis de La Galissonnière. Engraved by Hubert, 1780.

or goes out they must present arms and beat the drum. The governor-general has his own chapel where he offers prayers. . . .

AUGUST THE 15th

The new governor-general of all Canada, the Marquis de La Jonquière, arrived last night in the river before Quebec; but being late he reserved his public entrance for today . . . another great feast on account of the Ascension of the Virgin Mary. . . .

About eight o'clock the chief people in town assembled at the house of Mr. de Vaudreuil, who had lately been nominated governor of Trois Rivières and lived in the lower town, and whose father had likewise been governor-general of Canada. Thither came likewise the Marquis de la Galissonnière, who had till now been governor-general, and was to sail for France at the first opportunity. He was accompanied by all the people belonging to the government. I was likewise invited to see this festivity. At half an hour before eight the new governor-general went from the ship into a barge covered with red cloth. A signal with cannons was given from the ramparts for all the bells in town to be set ringing. All the people of distinction went down to the shore to salute the governor who, on alighting from the barge, was received by the Marquis de la Galissonnière. After they had saluted each other, the commandant of the town addressed the new governor in a very elegant speech which he answered very concisely. Then all the cannon on the ramparts gave a general salute. The whole street up to the cathedral was lined with men in arms, chiefly drawn from among the burgesses. The governor then walked towards the cathedral, dressed in a suit of red, with an abundance of gold lace. His servants went before him in green, carrying firearms on their shoulders. On his arrival at the cathedral he was received by the Bishop of Canada and the whole clergy assembled. The bishop was arrayed in his pontifical robes, and had a long gilt tiara on his head, and a great crozier in his hand. After the bishop had addressed a short speech to the governor-general, a priest brought a silver crucifix on a long stick

(two priests with lighted tapers in their hands, going on each side of it) to be kissed by the governor. The bishop and the priests then went through the long aisle up to the choir. The servants of the governor followed with their hats on, and arms on their shoulders. At last came the governor and his suite and after them a crowd of people. At the beginning of the choir the governor and the General de la Galissonnière, stopped before a chair covered with red cloth and stood there during the whole time of the celebration of the mass, which was celebrated by the bishop himself. From the church he went to the palace where the gentlemen of note in the town afterwards went to pay their respects to him. The members of the different orders with their respective superiors likewise came to him to testify their joy on account of his happy arrival. Among the numbers that came to visit none stayed to dine but those that were invited beforehand, among which I had the honor to be. The entertainment lasted very long, and was as elegant as the occasion required.[19]

From the Château the last two governors of New France watched the decline and fall of the colony. The Marquis Duquesne bungled his part in the Seven Years War; and the younger Vaudreuil, the only Canadian-born of his line, came into conflict with Montcalm in the defence of Quebec. Yet the old traditions were carried on to the end and were indeed to survive the French régime: the annual paying of homage by the seigneurs to the king's representative[20] and, most durable of all, the New Year's levée.

Then came the tragic events of 1759. Up to 25 June Montcalm was writing confidential letters to his friend Brigadier François-Charles de Bourlamaque — letters which reveal a polite dalliance on the general's part with the Marquise de Vaudreuil in the shadow of doom. "Brûlez cette lettre, — brûlez toutes mes lettres",[21] he enjoined his correspondent at the end of the letters.

Louisbourg

Île Royale, later to be named Cape Breton, had by the Treaty of Utrecht become the truncated base of French power on the Atlantic coast. A turbulent bay with a rocky beach was chosen as the site for a very large fortress intended to guard the mouth of the St Lawrence from British attack. Here in 1719, under the second governor of Île Royale, Joseph de Saint-Ovide, were begun the King's Bastion and Château of Louisbourg.[22] The military engineer François de Verville (d. 1729) designed the works on a peninsula jutting into the harbour. Construction by soldiers and artisans brought from France was difficult from the beginning, the weather and unsuitable local materials nearly defeating the best efforts of both Verville and his successor Étienne Verrier (1683-1747). But during the twelve years of their building, the bastion and the long two-storey Château in front of it gradually took shape.

Anonymous: Le Bastion du Roy . . . Louisbourg.

The Château of Louisbourg, reconstructed.

The Château consisted of two wings: the soldiers' barracks at the right as seen from the landing; at centre a graceful arcaded lantern with an obelisk spire over the portal and chapel of four bays, the chaplain's room, officers' quarters and, at the far end, the governor's pavilion. The unified and symmetrical design of this building with its elegant if restrained ornament exhibited much more of the character of contemporary French architecture than Frontenac's château at Quebec. But it was the architecture of the military establishments rather than that of the palaces of France. The Château was very largely finished by 1731.

The chapel interior, with its handsome carved oak retable, would have been entirely at home in provincial France. It was fully equipped with silver vessels and with hangings and Mass vestments in the liturgical colours. The governor occupied a stall near the altar and at Mass was the first after the clergy and acolytes to receive communion. The chapel, dedicated to St Louis, served the whole community until a parish church was built in the town.

The ground floor of the governor's pavilion contained four rooms of modest size: a vestibule, two rooms for the Superior Council (one of them doubling as a state dining room), and a serving room. On the first floor were the governor's dining room, study, bedroom and dressing room. The furnishings — *boiseries* of rococo design, tables covered with Turkey carpets, leather chairs, canopied bed, gilt mirrors, gaming-tables and French silver and porcelain — were brought from France and represented a high degree of luxury for their time and place. All the interiors have been faithfully restored during the reconstruction of Louisbourg which began in 1965.

Louisbourg's history, governed by events in the larger theatre of European politics and war, was but a brief one. The New England invasion of 1745 under Warren and Pepperell displaced the French and installed the British until 1749. True to type, the New Englanders made the chapel over into a preaching hall, removing the altar and building galleries and pews. These additions were in their turn removed as soon as the French regained possession by the provisions of the Treaty of Aix-la-Chapelle. French elegance returned to the Château in the form of the lavish dinners and entertainments held by the last two governors, the Comte de Raymond and Augustin de Drucourt.

All this came to an abrupt end in the summer of 1758. Amherst's force appeared at the approaches to Louisbourg in June, and within weeks the great fortress had fallen, as a prelude to Wolfe's capture of Quebec the following year. The French departed from the region forever. Charles Lawrence had already expelled the Acadians from the Nova Scotia mainland, and Monckton now ravaged the settlements on the St John River. Cape Breton became British, eventually to be annexed to Nova Scotia.

The Château of Louisbourg was heavily damaged in the fighting; but the governor's wing was reparable and seems to have been occupied until the British finally abandoned the place in 1768. After that, disintegration was rapid, owing to the weather and the plundering of building materials by the new inhabitants of the region, until in our own century very little remained above ground. But a wealth of material lay below for twentieth-century archaeologists to find. This, and the abundance of documentary material in the archives of France, made exact restoration possible. Much evidence has been found of the daily life of the Château and town, down to such articles as shoes and children's toys. The grave of one of the governors who died in the Château, Louis de Forant, and those of several officers were found beneath the chapel floor. The Louisbourg of today stands as a massive and exemplary reconstitution of an important chapter in Canadian history.

The Governor's Bedroom, Château of
Louisbourg, reconstructed.

Governors and Lieutenant Governors of Acadia

Pierre Du Gua de Monts (1558?-1628)	1603-1608
Jean de Biencourt de Poutrincourt et de Saint-Just (1591/2-1623)	1606-1614
Charles de Biencourt de Saint-Just (1591/2-1623/4)	1614-1623
Charles de Saint-Étienne de La Tour (1593-1666)	1631-1642 and 1653-1657
Isaac de Razilly (1587-1635)	1632-1635
Charles de Menou d'Aulnay (1604?-1650)	1638-1650
Emmanuel Le Borgne (1610-1675)	1657-1667
William Crowne (1617-1682) with	1662-1667
Sir Thomas Temple (1613/4-1674)	1662-1667
Alexandre Le Borgne de Belle-Isle (1640/3-c.1693)	1668-1670
Hector d'Andigné de Grandfontaine (1627-1696)	1670-1673
Jacques de Chambly (d.1687)	1673-1677
François-Marie Perrot (1644-1691)	1684-1687
Louis-Alexandre Des Friches de Meneval (fl.1687-1703)	1687-1690
Joseph Robinau de Villebon (1655-1700)	1691-1700
Jacques-François Mombeton de Brouillan (1651–1705)	1701-1705
Daniel d'Auger de Subercase (1661-1723)	1706-1710

Governors and Governors General of New France

Samuel de Champlain (c.1570-1635)	1612-1629 and 1633-1635
Charles Huault de Montmagny (c.1583-1653)	1636-1648
Louis d'Ailleboust de Coulonge et d'Argentenay (c.1612-1660)	1648-1651
Jean de Lauson (c.1584-1666)	1651-1657
Pierre Voyer d'Argenson, vicomte de Mouzay (1625-1709?)	1658-1661
Pierre Dubois Davaugour (d.1664)	1661-1663
Augustin de Saffray de Mézy (d.1665)	1663-1665
Daniel de Rémy de Courcelle (1626-1698)	1665-1672
Louis de Buade de Frontenac et de Palluau, comte (1622-1698)	1672-1682 and 1689-1698
Joseph-Antoine Le Febvre de La Barre (1622-1688)	1682-1685
Jacques-René de Brisay de Denonville (1637-1710)	1685-1689
Louis-Hector de Callière (1648-1703)	1698-1703
Philippe de Rigaud de Vaudreuil (c.1643-1725)	1703-1725
Charles de Beauharnois de la Boische, marquis de Beauharnois (1671-1749)	1726-1747
Roland-Michel Barrin de La Galissonière, marquis de La Galissonière (1693-1756)	1747-1749
Jacques-Pierre de Taffanel de La Jonquière, marquis de La Jonquière (1685-1752)	1749-1752
Ange Duquesne de Menneville, marquis Duquesne (c.1700-1778)	1752-1755
Pierre de Rigaud de Vaudreuil de Cavagnial, marquis de Vaudreuil (1698-1778)	1755-1760

Governors of Île Royale

Philippe Pastour de Costebelle (d.1717)	1713-1717
Joseph de Mombeton de Brouillan dit Saint-Ovide (1676-1755)	1718-1739
Isaac-Joseph de Forant (d.1740)	1739-1740
Jean-Baptiste-Louis Le Prévost Duquesnel (d.1744)	1740-1744
Sir Charles Knowles (1704-1777)	1747-1749
Charles Des Herbiers de la Ralière (c.1700-1752)	1749-1751
Jean-Louis de Raymond, comte de Raymond (1702-1771)	1751-1754
Augustin Boschenry de Drucourt (1703-1762)	1754-1758

Quebec and Lower Canada

Quebec 1760-1841
Spencer Wood/Bois de Coulonge

James Cockburn: Chateau St. Louis, Quebec *(the Château Haldimand at right). Water colour, 26 June 1829.*

Quebec 1760-1841

The Seven Years War left the French settlement on the St Lawrence and its vast inland empire in British hands. The population totalled only seventy thousand, five thousand of which lived in the capital city. After Wolfe's bombardment of Quebec in 1759 scarcely a building was left unscathed. The scale of the devastation is evident in Richard Short's series of engraved views of the city published in 1761. The Château Saint-Louis, perched on its cliff, suffered somewhat less than most buildings but was nevertheless in a ruinous state.[1] Amherst, who received the surrender of Montreal from Vaudreuil in 1760, and who assured the continuity of government and religion, paid only a brief visit to Quebec before disappearing from the Canadian scene. One of his staff, Colonel James Murray, who was fluent in French, was left behind as military governor of Quebec. After the Peace of Paris in 1763 Murray, now a general, became governor of Canada.

The following year Murray had the Château repaired in order to house his living quarters and offices. To judge from a drawing of 1804, the courtyard façade was somewhat altered.[2] At the Château, Murray in person held courts both civil and criminal. Soon, however, he came into conflict with the clique of merchants newly arrived from England and the Thirteen Colonies over his policy of perpetuating the legal system of New France over and against their commercial interests. The newcomers blackened his character, and he was recalled to England in 1766. Another former member of Amherst's staff, Guy (later Sir Guy) Carleton succeeded him, only to continue the old policy of reconciliation in the interests of maintaining domestic peace and securing the loyalty of Canadians to the British Crown. As a result he too came into conflict with the merchants, his stormiest session with his Council taking place just after Murray's departure.

He is said to have struck out wildly at the members during a dinner at the Château.

Yet life in Quebec had its pleasanter side. Frances Brooke, wife of the chaplain to the forces from 1765 to 1768, describes in *The History of Emily Montague* the amusements of the English community and their Canadian friends: the picnics at Montmorency and the balls at the Château ("all the world will be at the governor's"). In the light of Murray's affability and Carleton's intransigence, the meaning of a remark she puts into the mouth of one of her characters becomes clear: "It is astonishing, in a small community like this, how much depends on the personal character of him who governs".[3]

Anonymous: Sir Guy Carleton, 1st Lord Dorchester, c.1780.

For the Anglo-Americans, fuel was added to the fire by the Quebec Act of 1774, which established the French civil code and guaranteed toleration of Roman Catholicism. Despite his repulse of the American invasion under Montgomery and Arnold in 1775-6, and his convoking (at the Château) of an appointed Assembly in 1776, Carleton's opponents frustrated him to such an extent that he retired in 1778. But his policies prevailed and were largely responsible for the stability of the Québécois in the turbulent years of the American Revolution.

Carleton's successor was the Swiss-born British general, Sir Frederick Haldimand, who had formerly been commander-in-chief at Boston. In the Château Saint-Louis in 1782 he was visited by the young Horatio Nelson, then captain of H.M. Frigate *Albermarle*. It was in Nelson's character promptly to fall in love with a Quebec beauty of sixteen, Mary Simpson,

James Cockburn: Quebec — Place d'Armes *(the rear of the Château Haldimand at centre). Water colour, 1829.*

whom he had to leave behind on his departure; she later married the governor of the Chelsea Hospital in London.[4] Also on record is Haldimand's "grand ball and supper" on the Queen's birthday in 1784, for it was this function, held on a Sunday, that was blamed by the clergy for a gale which carried off the crosses of several churches.

By this time the Château was badly in need of further repairs. These were effected between 1784 and 1786; but more were needed. The capital had increased in population, and the space available to the governor for his official duties and social functions was severely limited. Accordingly in 1786 Haldimand built an annexe to the Château as a separate building across the courtyard.[5] This "Château Haldimand" utilized a part of an old wall of the old fort and was thus windowless at the rear of its ground floor. More than that, it was a plain building of Quebec design, with massive chimneys, and lacked ornament of any kind. But good use was made of the large assembly-rooms it contained, which were said to be the best in Canada for dancing. The governor continued, however, to live in the old Château. A popular and beautiful visitor in 1781, the Baroness Frederika von Riedesel, wife of the general commanding the German mercenaries in the American Revolution, remarked on the rooms "furnished and arranged after the English fashion" and Haldimand's garden "full of fruits and foreign plants".[5a]

The patched-up Château gradually deteriorated. Its rooms were small and primitive by the standards of the day. Consequently Carleton, on his return in 1786 as Lord Dorchester and Governor-in-Chief of British North America, chose to live in Haldimand's new house, relegating the old building to his council and staff. The following year, in the one house or the other, he received the boisterous young Prince William Henry, Duke of Clarence, who had arrived in H.M.

Frigate *Pegasus.* Dinner was served at four in the afternoon and a ball followed at six or seven. To Dorchester's dismay the future King William IV, having perfunctorily danced with the important ladies, plain or downright ugly, spent the rest of the evening with the pretty ones.[6] A display of fireworks was also held for him in the Citadel. In 1794 another royal entertainment took place, this time a levée for Prince Edward, later Duke of Kent, who had just returned to Quebec from Martinique along with his regiment and his beautiful mistress Julie de Saint-Laurent. Several years earlier, in December 1791, Mrs Simcoe, wife of the lieutenant governor of Upper Canada, had written in her diary of "a very pleasant Ball at the Chateau & danced with Prince Edward".[7] Yet another visitor in Dorchester's time was a dashing young Irish nephew of the Duke of Richmond, Lord Edward Fitzgerald,* who had performed the feat of walking the whole of the way from Fredericton to Quebec in the winter. But all was not frivolity, for it was in the old Château that Dorchester presided over the founding of the Quebec Agricultural Society in 1789.

In the period of Robert Prescott, governor from 1796 to 1807, the usual entertainments were held, among them a dance in the old Château of the sort that is illustrated in a drawing by George Heriot. The dancing takes place in a plain plastered room with a beamed ceiling, in which the only eighteenth-century touches are a rococo mirror on the wall and curtains hung in swags over the small-paned windows. A

A son of the 1st Duke of Leinster, he served in the army until 1792, when he was cashiered for attending a revolutionary meeting in Paris. He was later arrested after preparing a plan for an Irish uprising and died in Newgate Prison.

George Heriot: Dance in the Chateau St. Louis. *Detail of a water colour, 1801.*

contemporary English opinion of this traditional architecture of Quebec is voiced by Isaac Weld, the traveller who visited the city in August 1796:

> The chateau, wherein the governor resides, is a plain building of common stone, situated in an open place, the houses around which form three sides of an open square. It consists of two parts. The old and the new are separated from each other by a spacious court. The former stands just on the verge of an inaccessible rock: behind it, on the outside, there is a long gallery from which, if a pebble were let drop, it would fall at least sixty feet perpendicularly. The old part is chiefly taken up with public offices, and all the apartments in it are small and ill contrived; but in the new part, which stands in front of the other, facing the square, they are very spacious and tolerably well furnished, but none of them can be called elegant. This part is inhabited by the governor's family. The chateau is built without any regularity or design, neither the old nor the new having even a uniform front. . . . Every morning during summer, one of the regiments of the garrison parades in the open place before the chateau, and the band plays for an hour or two, at which time the place becomes the resort of numbers of the most genteel people of the town, and has a very gay appearance.[8]

In 1808, the population of Quebec having swelled considerably and the province having been divided into Upper and Lower Canada by the Constitutional Act of

1791, the Legislature at last undertook a major reconstruction of the Château Saint-Louis. In these years the dictatorial Sir James Craig, who had fought under Burgoyne in the American Revolution, was Governor-in-Chief of Canada. He was the first to occupy the completed Château, if only for a few months before his departure in 1811. He was succeeded by the francophile Sir George Prevost, that "tiny, light, gossamer man", who in the War of 1812 personally led an unsuccessful action against the Americans.

The designer of the reconstruction is not on record, but the particular combination which the finished building exhibited, of the English Palladian and Quebec French styles, is the hallmark of the leading Quebec architect of his time, François Baillairgé (1759-1830). It would have been only natural to call on him as the first in Quebec after the Conquest to have studied in Paris. An unsigned and undated drawing which survives shows a central pavilion with a pediment containing a circular window, and below this a Palladian window. The two-storey building in the drawing restores symmetry to the Château, not only by creating a broad central pavilion, which masks five of the old bays and the old turret but by making the end wings into pedimented pavilions. The new main door is accented by side-lights and a little classic porch.

This scheme was carried out, but with the addition of an extra storey and a second-floor Palladian window. Smaller and lower wings, added at either end of the building, considerably lengthened the courtyard façade. The flattened roofs of the Classic Revival replaced the steep French ones of the original château.

The finished product is illustrated in several water-colour drawings of 1829 and 1830 by Colonel James Cockburn (1778/9-1847),[9] commandant of the Royal Artillery at Quebec. The plastered stone walls were colour-washed a light yellow, and the roof was covered Quebec-style with tin oxidized to a tile-red.[10] The total aspect of the restored Château, together with the Château Haldimand, is described by the Canadian geographer Joseph Bouchette (1774-1841) in terms markedly different from those of Isaac Weld sixteen years previously:

> The Castle of St. Louis, being the most prominent object on the summit of the rock, will obtain the first notice: it is a handsome stone building, seated near the edge of a precipice something more than two hundred feet high, and supported towards the steep by a solid work of masonry, rising nearly half the height of the edifice, and surmounted by a spacious gallery, from whence there is a most commanding prospect over the basin, the Island of Orleans, Point Levi, and the surrounding country. The whole is one hundred and sixty-two feet long, by forty-five broad, and three stories high: but in the direction of the Cape it has the appearance of being much more lofty; each extremity is

Anonymous: Project for the Courtyard Elevation of the Château Saint-Louis. Drawing, c.1808.

Sir John Watson Gordon: George Ramsay, 9th Earl of Dalhousie.

terminated by a small wing, giving the whole an easy and regular character: the interior arrangement is convenient, the decorative part tasteful and splendid, suitable in every respect for the residence of the governor-general.

. . . on the opposite side stands an extensive building, divided among the various offices of government both civil and military; it contains also a handsome suite of apartments, wherein the balls and other public entertainments of the court are always given. During the dilapidated state of the Chateau, this building was occupied by the family of the governors. Both exterior and interior are in a very plain style.[11]

Bouchette also mentions one "well stocked garden", 180 by seventy yards, and another 107 by seven yards.

James Cockburn: Chateau St. Louis, Quebec *(the* Château Haldimand *at left). Water colour, 26 June 1829.*

The Château Haldimand continued to be used for the state functions held by Prevost's successor Sir John Sherbrooke. Here, in 1818 and 1819, the Duke of Richmond lived up to his reputation for princely hospitality by holding the dances, concerts and plays described by Eliza-Anne Baby, the cultivated widow of Charles Casgrain. At one of the balls, the aged Ignace-Louis de Salaberry, who had fought with Burgoyne at Saratoga, appeared in the court dress in which he had been presented at the court of Louis XVI of France.[12] But it was in the old Château that the Duke's body lay in state in September 1810 after having been brought back from the wilderness near the Ottawa River, where he had died presumably of a rabid fox's bite.

Lord Dalhousie on his arrival in June 1820, fresh from the handsome Government House in Halifax, found the Château Saint-Louis in a "filthy state" and "miserably furnished" with the cast-offs of his predecessors.[13] But he managed to hold there the meetings which resulted in the founding of the Literary and Historical Society of Quebec and in the erection of the monument to Wolfe and Montcalm in the Governor's Garden.[14] But by the time of the ball he held to celebrate the coronation of King George IV, renovations had been carried out. Also in the old Château, Alexander Galt presented in Dalhousie's presence one of his own plays, a comedy about American visitors to Quebec.

The feminine note is struck in Lady Aylmer's diary[15] when she speaks of the old Château. Her husband became governor general in 1831, and on their arrival she was enchanted by the lofty site of their residence. The diary includes a plan of both principal floors, probably drawn by their friend Colonel James Cockburn. The ground floor contained the hall with a circular stair, sitting room, dining room and offices, the aide-de-camp's room, steward's quarters, a plate room and pantry. Upstairs were two drawing rooms, a billiards room and the Aylmers' bedroom, dressing room and bath as well as studies for the governor and his secretary. No plan is given of the second floor, which doubtless included additional bedrooms, servants' quarters and storerooms. She complains of the black horsehair sofas and of the uniform buff colour of the walls in the drawing rooms, but this is made up for by the magnificent view from the windows. By her time a greenhouse had been added to the Château.

In 1834, the year before the Aylmers departed, a terrible fire in the dead of winter destroyed the Château Saint-Louis so completely that nothing was left but ruins to be cleared away. All that remained was the famous terrace. It was enlarged in Lord Durham's

After Sir Thomas Lawrence: The Earl of Durham. *Copy, 1908, of the portrait of 1829.*

Lady Mary Lambton (later Countess of Elgin): Library Govt House Quebec. *Water colour, 31 October 1838.*

Lady Mary Lambton (later Countess of Elgin): L.M.L's Bedroom — Quebec. *Water colour, 1838.*

Lady Mary Lambton (later Countess of Elgin): Schoolroom (Government House, Quebec). *Water colour, 31 October 1838.*

time and named in his honour. The Château Haldi-mand was the only house available to the governor general. The Irish Whig, Lord Gosford, occupied it from 1835 to 1837 and there entertained Louis-Joseph Papineau shortly before the Rebellion of 1837 broke out. Gosford's attempt to conciliate the great Rebel having failed, he resigned his post.

In Lord Durham's single year in office, during which he made his survey of the two Canadas, he and his family lived for most of the time in temporary quarters in the Legislative building but held their receptions in the Château Haldimand. Their daughter Lady Mary Lambton, the future Lady Elgin, made charming drawings of the rooms in their private quarters, including the library, her schoolroom and a bedroom. Durham's successors, when they returned to Quebec during the government's sojournings elsewhere, occupied various rented quarters until the move was made to Spencer Wood in Elgin's time.

In the intervals during which the capital, after the Union of 1841, peregrinated to Kingston (1841-1844), to Montreal (1844-1849), to Toronto (1849-1852 and 1856-1859) and back to Quebec (1852-1855 and 1860-1865), the Château Haldimand was used for various purposes including government and city offices and as studios for the painter Antoine Plamondon and the architect Charles Baillairgé. By 1857 it had become the École normale Laval[16] which was its final state until it was demolished in 1892 to make way for the giant railway hotel, the Château Frontenac.

In Montreal the Château de Ramezay, an old governor's residence dating from the time of the elder Vaudreuil, was in use during the sojourn of 1844-9. Dickens, on his visit to Canada in 1842, had admired this modest house as "very superior to that at Kingston".[17] But in Lord Elgin's day Monklands, a late eighteenth-century villa on the outskirts, was leased as a "country Government House" (as a dashing young A.D.C. Lord Mark Kerr called it) though in the winter snowdrifts often isolated the house.[17a] Here were entertained all the political leaders including the former Rebels of 1837-8. It was here that Elgin retreated after the burning of the Legislature and his stoning by an angry mob in March 1849 after he had assented to the Rebellion Losses Bill. After these episodes the capital was moved to Toronto. A pleasan-ter side to life at Monklands is reflected in the dedication of a "Monklands Polka"* to Lady Alice Lambton, Lady Elgin's sister.

Dickens also visited Quebec, which in 1842 was bereft of its status of capital. Surpassing all his other outpourings on America is his rhapsody on "this Gibraltar of Canada: its giddy heights; its citadel suspended, as it were, in the air; its picturesque steep streets and frowning gateways . . . a place not to be forgotten or mixed up in the mind with other places."

It is mainly [he continues] in the prospect from the site of the Old Government House, and from the citadel,

*Another piece of sheet-music, "The Elgin Polka", was published in Montreal at about the same time; both are in the possession of the present Earl of Elgin.

that its surpassing beauty lies. The exquisite expanse of country, rich in field and forest, mountain-height and water, which lies stretched out before the view, with miles of Canadian village, glancing in long white streaks, like veins along the landscape; the motley crowd of gables, roofs, and chimney tops in the old hilly town immediately at hand; the beautiful St. Lawrence sparkling and flashing in the sunlight; and the tiny ships below the rock from which you gaze, whose distant rigging looks like spiders' webs against the light, while casks and barrels on their decks dwindle into toys, and busy mariners become so many puppets.[18]

If the Château is long gone, the view remains. It is one of the most majestic in the world.

The Château Haldimand, Quebec, as École normale Laval, before 1892.

Monklands, Montreal. Photograph by William Notman.

Spencer Wood/Bois de Coulonge

When the capital of Canada returned to Quebec in 1852 a new solution was sought to the old problem of a fitting residence for the governor general. It was found on the bank of the St Lawrence near the village of Sillery. Here, at a distance of two miles from the city walls of Quebec, a villa had been built about 1790 for Brigadier-General Henry Watson Powell, who had served under Carleton during the American Revolution. The land on which Powell Place stood had originally formed a part of Coulonge, the manor (*châtellenie*) which Louis d'Ailleboust had bought and to which he retired in 1651. On it he had built a house and farm buildings which apparently were still standing as late as 1738.[19]

Powell's house, as it appears in a water colour of 1830 by James Cockburn, was evidently a replacement. This "ample mansion"[20] was a handsome Palladian villa of a type inspired by the designs of James Gibbs, published in London in 1782. It occupied a magnificent site high above the river and was set in the "parklike grounds, with a noble avenue leading to the house" which reminded Cockburn of England.[21] True to the English ideal of the Picturesque, it stood out like a temple from its wooded setting. Its rectangular plan, classical cornice, portico and quoins, and pediment over the entrance were all features of the English Georgian. Yet for all its Englishness the house had a distinctly Canadian flavour arising from its casement windows and the planarity of its façade, so that like the enlarged Château Saint-Louis it suggests the hand of François Baillairgé. Inside, on the ground floor,[22] were four large rooms opening into a central hall, the domestic offices being relegated to separate small pavilions connected to the house by covered passages. There was also a small summerhouse or "kiosk".

Here Powell seems to have entertained the Duke of Kent and Madame de Saint-Laurent; and Mrs Simcoe attended several country parties in 1794 and 1795.[23] A later governor, Sir James Craig, leased it from its new owner (Powell had sold it in 1797) in the summers from 1807 to 1810, in order to ease his gout and dropsy. On its lawns he held the *fêtes champêtres* and alfresco dances which are described in the *Mémoires* of Philippe Aubert de Gaspé:

> At half-past eight A.M., on a bright August morning . . . the *élite* of the Quebec *beau monde* left the city to attend Sir James Craig's kind invitation. Once opposite Powell Place . . . the guests left their vehicles on the main road, and plunged into a dense forest, following a serpentine avenue which led to a delightful cottage in full view of the majestic St. Lawrence; the river here appears to flow past amidst luxurious green bowers which line its banks. Small tables for four, for six, for eight guests are laid out facing the cottage, on a platform of planed deals — this will shortly serve as a dancing floor *al fresco;* as the guests successively arrive, they form in parties to partake of a déjeuner *en famille.*

SPENCER WOOD, QUEBEC, 1829.

James Cockburn: Spencer Wood. *Water colour, 1829.*

I say *en famille*, for an *aide-de-camp* and a few waiters excepted, no one interferes with the small groups clubbed together to enjoy their early repast, of which cold meat, radishes, bread, tea and coffee form the staples. Those whose appetites are appeased make room for new comers, and amuse themselves strolling under the shade of trees. At ten the cloth is removed; the company are all on the *qui vive* . . . a few minutes elapse, and the chief entrance is thrown open; little King Craig followed by a brilliant staff, enters. Simultaneously an invisible orchestra, located high amidst the dense foliage of large trees, strikes up "God Save the King". . . . The magnates press forward to pay their respects to His Excellency. Those who do not

George Heriot: Fête Given by Sir James Craig at Spencer Wood. *Watercolour drawing, 1809.*

*Frederick P. Rubidge: Elevations of
Spencer Wood. Drawing, 1851.*

intend to "trip the light fantastic toe" take seats on the platform where His Excellency sits in state; an A.D.C. calls out, *gentlemen, take your partners,* and the dance begins. . . .

It is half-past two in the afternoon; we are gaily going through the figures of a country-dance, "Speed the plough" perhaps, when the music stops short; everyone is taken aback, and wonders at the cause of the interruption. The arrival of two prelates, Bishop Plessis and Bishop Mountain, gave us the solution of the enigma; an aide-de-camp had mentioned to the band-master to stop on noticing the arrival of the two high dignitaries of the respective churches. The dance was interrupted whilst they were there, and was resumed on their departure. Sir James had introduced this point of etiquette from the respect he entertained for their persons.
At three the loud sound of a hunter's horn is heard in the distance; all follow His Excellency in a path cut through the then virgin forest of Powell Place. Some of the guests from the length of the walk, began to think that Sir James had intended those who had not danced to take a "constitutional" before dinner, when, on rounding an angle a huge table, canopied with green boughs, groaning under the weight of dishes, struck on their view. . . . Nothing could exceed in magnificence, in sumptuousness this repast — such was the opinion not only of Canadians, for whom such displays were new, but also of the European guests, though there was a slight drawback to the perfect enjoyment of the dishes — *the materials which composed them we could not recognize,* so great was the artistic skill, so wonderful the manipulations of Monsieur Petit, the French cook.

The Bishops left about half an hour after dinner, when dancing was resumed with an increasing ardor, but the cruel mammas were getting concerned respecting certain sentimental walks which the daughters were enjoying after sunset. They ordered them home, if not with their menacing attitude with which the goddess Calypso is said to have spoken to her nymphs, at least

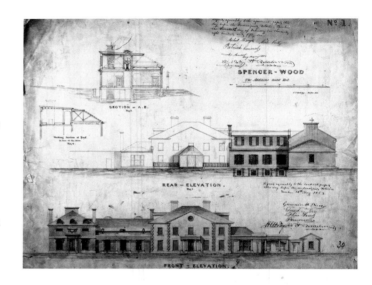

with frowns; so said the gay young *cavaliers.* By nine o'clock, all had re-entered Quebec.[24]

Greater fame came to the place after it had been sold, once again, in 1815, to Michael Henry Perceval, collector of customs at Quebec, who renamed it Spencer Wood in honour of an exalted uncle, Spencer Perceval, the British prime minister who had been assassinated in 1812. At Perceval's invitation the Duke of Richmond rambled and picnicked in the grounds with his family; and Lord Dalhousie after him botanized with the Percevals' beautiful neighbour Mrs Peter Sheppard of Woodfield. Both house and grounds attracted the attention of the artists who visited Quebec. Perceval entertained all of Quebec society: the Uniackes, de Gaspés and Babys, at his musical parties, dinners and dances.

In 1833 the property was sold once more. The buyer was Henry Atkinson, a Quebec merchant, whose "improvements" began the transformation of the house into a rustic seat according to the tastes of a new generation. The grounds became an even greater attraction than before. Atkinson hired an English gardener, Peter Lowe, to lay them out in the Romantic manner, with a sweeping vista to the river, a wood with glades where wild flowers grew and gardens stocked with exotic plants. The hothouses contained orchids and the peaches and pineapples which were ripened for Christmas. In 1842 the owner conducted John James Audubon through the grounds and named one of his paths for the great ornithological artist.[25] Spencer Wood gained a wider fame when it was described in several of the English gardening periodicals. Sir James Le Moine, writing from memory, sums up the Spencer Wood of his earlier days:

> It was then a splendid old seat of more than one hundred acres, a fit residence for the proudest noble-man England might send as Viceroy — enclosed east and west between two streamlets, hidden from the highway by a dense growth of oak, maple, dark pines and firs — the forest primeval — letting in here and there the light of heaven on its labyrinthine avenues; a most striking landscape, blending the sombre verdure of its hoary trees with the soft tints of its velvety sloping lawn, fit for a ducal palace. An elfish plot of a flower garden, alas! how much dwarfed, then stood in rear of the dwelling to the north; it once enjoyed the privilege of attracting many eyes. It had also an extensive and well-kept fruit and vegetable garden, enlivened with the loveliest possible circular fount in white marble, supplied with the crystal element from the Belle-Borne rill by a hidden aqueduct; conservato-ries, graperies, peach and forcing houses, pavilions picturesquely hung over the yawning precipice on two headlands, one looking towards Sillery, the other towards the Island of Orleans, the scene of many a cosy tea-party; bowers, rustic chairs *perdues* among the groves, a superb bowling green and archery grounds. The mansion itself contained an exquisite collection of paintings from old masters, a well-selected library of rare and standard works, illuminated Roman missals,

rich portfolios with curious etchings, marble busts, quaint statuettes, medals and medallions, *objets de vertu* purchased by the millionaire proprietor during a four year's residence in Italy, France and Germany. Such we remember Spencer Wood in its palmiest days.[26]

Spencer Wood now inspired literary outpourings. In 1848 a visitor from Brighton inscribed an envoi in Atkinson's daughter's album:

> Thy classic lawn, with its antiquated oaks and solemn pines, thy wood-crowned cliffs and promontories, with sparkling sunlight reflected . . . from the broad surface of Jacques Cartier's river, hundreds of feet below. And then the quiet repose of thy ample mansion, with its stores of art and models of taste within and without; thy forest glades, thy gardens, thy flowers and thy fruit. But most of all, thy gay and happy inmates, their glad and joyous hearts beating with generous emotions, and their countenances brightened with the welcome smile. Ah! how I seem to hear, as in time past I have heard, their lively prattle, or their merry laugh echoing across the lawns, or through the flower garden, or along the winding paths down the steep slope to the pavilion.[27]

But it was left to an irresponsible young Irish-Canadian poet, Adam Kidd (1802-1831) to foretell the future:

> Through thy green groves and deep receding bowers,
> Loved Spencer Wood! how often have I strayed,
> Or mused away the calm, unbroken hours,
> Beneath some broad oak's cool, refreshing shade.
>   . . .
> But soon, how soon, a different scene I trace,
> Where I have wandered, or oft musing stood;
> And those whose cheering looks enhanced the place,
> No more shall smile on thee, lone Spencer Wood.[28]

It was Spencer Wood which was chosen in 1852 as a residence for Lord Elgin. Over the next few years the house was enlarged to the designs of the Public Works

After Sir Francis Grant: James Bruce, 8th Earl of Elgin. Copy, 1907.

Spencer Wood/Bois de Coulonge, Quebec: the River Front. Photograph by Livernois, 1871.

architect Frederick Preston Rubidge (1806-1898). Photographs reveal even further modifications which transformed the house into a long rambling affair, by the addition of continuous verandas supported on posts. These verandas gave it a horizontal aspect and caused it to nestle into, rather than contrast with, the landscape. With the original villa scarcely visible beneath the accretions, the change was complete from the Classic taste of the eighteenth century to the Romantic of the nineteenth.[29]

In September 1852 a young English traveller came to Spencer Wood armed with a letter of introduction to Lord Elgin. He was Henry Arthur Bright, a member of a shipping firm in Birmingham, and educated at Rugby and Cambridge. Elgin took to him and asked him to dinner one evening:

James Bruce, 8th Earl of Elgin, who had arrived as governor general in 1847, was the son of the collector of the Elgin Marbles. He loved Spencer Wood and extended its hospitality in the form of dinners served by footmen in powdered wigs. Complaints of his extravagance were voiced from Opposition benches in the Legislature, occupied by the "Clear Grits". But these latter were equally critical of one Legislative dinner at which pork and beans, sauerkraut and pumpkin pie were served,[30] perhaps in an attempt on the part of the Governor General to placate his critics.

> The drive up to the House was pretty, as far as we could judge of it. Torches on the trees partially lit it up, and showed us soldiers pacing along before the house, and at the gates. The house is of wood, and though nicely furnished, the rooms look small and rather beneath the dignity of the Queen's representative. We were received by Colonel Bruce* . . . who after a few words to set us at our ease, turned to receive the others. Luckily our friends the Speaker and Mr. Langton** were there, so that we did very well, and were both busily talking when His Excellency entered. There was at once silence, and he came round shaking hands with us all, and staying some time with the Speaker and Burder;*** his only decoration was the Star of the Thistle, which glistened on his breast, while the green ribband of the Order crossed from left to right across his waistcoat . . . . It was a pleasant, though a good, rather than a grand dinner, with not wonderful wine. The plate was beautiful, and for the first time in my life I eat soup, fish, etc. out of silver, dessert out of gold plate! Lord E. talked much and well, getting excited after dinner on the subject of Canada, and having quite a long discussion with Mr. Crawford opposite, while the English M.P. . . . patronized the Canadians and Lord Elgin, and behaved like an important snob as he is. Lord Elgin said, "I wish you all to be *proud* of being Canadians — Canadians in heart and feeling".[31]

The talk ranged from Elgin's recent visit to Boston and his meeting with the American president, to his conversations with Papineau, who by this time was back in the Assembly.[32]

The Governor General's younger brother, who acted as his secretary.
**M.L.A. for Peterborough and later Auditor General.*
***Bright's Cambridge friend and travelling companion*

A few days later Bright breakfasted at Spencer Wood. In the "pretty drawing-room adorned with pictures of the good lord himself and his children" he met Lady Elgin and a young Lambton cousin. He heard from the Governor General the whole story of the Rebellion Losses Bill and the stoning in Montreal. In the course of a walk in the grounds, to a point where they were looking across to the cliffs of Quebec — to Bright a scene "altogether to *me* the most splendid I ever saw" — Elgin said to him:

> One thing the removal of the seat of Government to Toronto and Quebec has done; it has shown the Lower Canadians that there is in the Upper Province as high a cultivation and as fine a country as any in the United States. It has shown the Upper Canadians this glorious rock and made them proud of possessing it.

After three hours Bright left, "having talked all the time, the kind old man walking us round to see his place — and a charming place it is, worthy of its possessor".[33]

Lord Elgin's years at Spencer Wood ended in 1854. In a valedictory address delivered after his most recent return to the place, he revealed his affection for it:

> I mounted the hill and drove through the avenue to the house door. I saw the drooping trees on the lawn, with every one of which I was so familiar, clothed in the tenderest green of spring, and the river beyond calm and transparent as a mirror.[34]

He was succeeded by the scholarly Sir Edmund Head, whose considerable success as lieutenant governor of New Brunswick had led to his appointment as governor general. An early advocate of British North American union, he had recommended the backwoods city of Ottawa as the compromise capital of Canada.

At Spencer Wood, on a February evening in 1860, Head was to have held one of his weekly Legislative dinners, with John A. Macdonald, George-Etienne Cartier and other leaders of the government in

attendance. As the guests were arriving fire broke out and in several hours the house was utterly destroyed. This happened only months before the visit of the young Albert Edward, Prince of Wales (the future King Edward VII). The Heads moved into Cataraqui, a neighbouring villa, and there held their various entertainments for the prince, who was put up in rooms in the Legislative Building. The traditional visits were paid to the Ursuline Convent and the Université Laval and addresses were received from all organizations in the city. The Governor General, wearing the Windsor uniform for public occasions, accompanied the Prince on the ensuing tour of Canada.

The rebuilding of Spencer Wood, to new designs by Rubidge, commenced the following year, just before the arrival of Lord Monck, the quiet Irish peer who was to press hard for Confederation and to inaugurate the new nation in 1867. He and his family

Henry Weigall: Sir Edmund Walker Head, Bt, 1866.

Spencer Wood/Bois de Coulonge, Quebec: the River Front with Verandas. Photograph c.1961.

lived in various quarters in Quebec until the new Spencer Wood was finished in the spring of 1863.[35] In spite of what some considered to be its "niggardly" and barracks-like appearance and consequent lack of symbolic value, the new house pleased its occupants by its modern comforts; and it avoided the excesses of Victorian design. Its design was in fact simple in the extreme: a large, plain two-storey brick building, clapboarded against the weather, with a central block projecting out very slightly on the river front. The whole was covered with a low-pitched roof.

Running the length of the river front was a veranda which was screened in with mosquito netting during the summers. A *porte-cochère* of Italianate design on the road front and a greenhouse attached to one end of the house completed the exterior arrangements.[36] In the grounds were lodges for the secretary, porter and coachman, a farm, an icehouse, coach house, stables, rackets court, skating rink, toboggan slide, croquet lawn and cricket field.

Indoors,[37] the rooms were made comfortable with many Victorian marble fireplaces and quantities of florid Rococo Revival furniture, with chandeliers and porcelain from France and silver from England. On the ground floor were the entrance hall with its green marble table, the state drawing room with grand piano and "Etruscan" vases, the state dining room with a table seating fifty, a small dining room and a billiards room. Upstairs a range of bedrooms included the governor's suite with its bird's-eye maple furniture.

The Monck family greatly enjoyed their country seat. In it they entertained an ever-increasing number of visitors, including several royal princes. Lord Lyons, the British ambassador to Washington, came in 1864 to discuss the threat of American invasion by a victorious Northern army after the Civil War. Tom Thumb of Barnum's travelling circus, the London journalist-traveller George Augustus Sala, and the American Civil War generals Sherman and Grant were among the others. The delegates to the Quebec Conference of 1864 were dined at Spencer Wood during the deliberations which paved the way to Confederation. One evening, during Lord Lyons's visit, the Governor General entered the drawing room to find that pandemonium had broken loose because family cats had pounced on a dog belonging to the Bishop's daughter. The guests "flew in all directions".[38]

Meanwhile, in 1858, the remote lumbering town of Ottawa (formerly Bytown) had been proclaimed capital of Canada, as Queen Victoria's choice among the other competitors for the honour. New parliament buildings had been designed the following year. Wrangling ensued over the impending move to the backwoods and it was not until 1865 that the civil servants began moving their desks to Ottawa. Monck and his family were loath to leave their beloved Spencer Wood when obliged to stay for short times in the small villa which had been rented for them on the banks of the Rideau River. It was only after Rideau Hall had been added to and made to resemble Spencer Wood as closely as possible that they became reconciled to it. Rideau Hall also received an Italianate porch, a greenhouse and a cricket field which were the duplicates of those in Quebec.[39]

Spencer Wood was retained for a few years after 1867 as a refuge from Ottawa for the governor general. But in 1870 it was given over to the province of Quebec as the residence of its lieutenant governor. The first occupant under the new régime was Sir Narcisse Belleau who remained in office long enough to receive the third governor general of Canada, Lord Dufferin, and his wife, who were charmed by the house. Successive lieutenant governors, though creatures of the federal government, and therefore usually former politicians, nevertheless included men of cultivation, who upheld the viceregal style of Spencer Wood. The unstable Letellier de Saint-Just held *soirées littéraires* before he, an old Liberal who was anathema to the clerical party, interfered in the Conservative provincial government and was dismissed by Macdonald; but his successor Théodore Robitaille carried on the old tradition by holding concerts and "artistic" evenings.

As for the Governor General of Canada, he now lacked a residence in the ancient capital. Lord Dufferin remedied this situation by setting up summer quarters in one of the Regency buildings in the Citadel of Quebec. These quarters were cramped and ill-furnished until they were enlarged under the Marquess of Lorne, and indeed until in 1928 they were made suitable for occupation in all seasons under Lord Willingdon. Every governor general to the present day has enjoyed

them. Meanwhile, in 1875, Dufferin had engaged an Irish architect William Lynn to design a huge new Château Saint-Louis in baronial style within the Citadel.[40] This grandiose project was fortunately never realized.

In 1893 Lady Aberdeen, wife of the governor general of that day, greatly admired Spencer Wood and mentioned in her diary a suggestion that had been made to recover the property from the province — but thought that this would be a great mistake. She found the lieutenant governor of the period, Sir Joseph-Adolphe Chapleau, to be "a very cultivated man and most pleasant to talk to" and his French "delightful to listen to".[41]

Government House, Quebec. Photograph c.1967.

Their Honours Gilles Lamontagne and Mme Lamontagne at Government House, Quebec. Photograph 1984.

Over the years Spencer Wood acquired further additions and underwent many refurbishings, most of these latter prompted by impending royal visits. Thus a substantial service wing was built in preparation for the Duke and Duchess of Cornwall and York (the future George V and Queen Mary). On their visit in 1901 a splendid party was held, and another such for the Prince's second visit in 1908, as Prince of Wales, to inaugurate the tercentenary celebrations of the founding of Quebec.

Gradually a library was accumulated, well stocked with Canadiana and the French and English classics. Some years later, under Narcisse Pérodeau, the furnishings included a sculpture by Rodin. A chapel was formed by joining two of the bedrooms. The coach house contained a large number of carriages and sleighs. Early in the present century the garden front of the house was lent dignity by the replacement of the old veranda with a Classic colonnade and, in 1916, given an official character by a monumental Doric portico *à l'américaine*,[42] so that Spencer Wood now appeared as a white castle when seen from the river.

Changes in the furniture over the years reflected the tastes of the times and of successive occupants: a player-piano was replaced by a gramophone and still later by radio and television. But the Victorian splendour of the interiors remained to the end. King George VI and Queen Elizabeth stayed in 1939. General de Gaulle came in 1960, by which time the place had reverted to its ancient name of Bois de Coulonge. The Quebec literary group Les Dix were accorded viceregal recognition and were entertained regularly from the 1930s. Paintings and sculptures lent by the Musée du Québec enhanced the Quebec flavour of the house.

Another great fire sealed the fate of the house. On a winter night in 1966 the lieutenant governor, Paul Comtois, himself perished in the flames which completely destroyed Bois de Coulonge. Since the appointment of Hugues Lapointe in 1967, the lieutenant governors of Quebec have occupied a comfortable modern house in the Chemin Saint-Louis not far from the gates of the old house. The rebuilding of Bois de Coulonge has been contemplated but not yet accomplished; but the famous grounds have remained open to the public.

Spencer Wood/Bois de Coulonge,
Quebec. Photograph c.1961.

H.M. The Queen and Prince Philip with Paul Comtois (right), Lieutenant Governor, at the entrance of Bois de Coulonge, Quebec, 1964.

QUEBEC & LOWER CANADA

Governors and Governors General of Quebec, British North America and Canada 1760-1867

James Murray (1721/2-1784)	1760-1768
Sir Guy Carleton, 1st Baron Dorchester (1724-1808)	1768-1778 and 1786-1796
Sir Frederick Haldimand (1718-1791)	1778-1786
Robert Prescott (1725-1816)	1796-1807
Sir James Henry Craig (1748-1812)	1807-1811
Sir George Prevost, Bt (1767-1816)	1811-1815
Sir John Coape Sherbrooke (1764-1830)	1816-1818
Charles Gordon Lennox, 4th Duke of Richmond (1764-1819)	1818-1819
George Ramsay, 9th Earl of Dalhousie (1770-1838)	1819-1828
Matthew Whitworth-Aylmer, 5th Baron Aylmer (1775-1850)	1831-1835
Archibald Acheson, 1st Earl of Gosford (1776-1849)	1835-1838
John George Lambton, 1st Earl of Durham (1792-1840)	1838
Sir John Colborne, later 1st Baron Seaton (1778-1863)	1839
Charles Poulett Thomson, 1st Baron Sydenham (1799-1841)	1839-1841
Sir Charles Bagot, Bt (1781-1843)	1841-1843
Sir Charles Theophilus Metcalfe, 1st Baron Metcalfe (1785-1846)	1843-1845
Charles Murray Cathcart, 2nd Earl of Cathcart (1783-1859)	1846-1847
James Bruce, 8th Earl of Elgin (1811-1863)	1847-1854
Sir Edmund Walker Head (1805-1868)	1854-1861
Sir Charles Stanley Monck, 4th Viscount Monck (1819-1894)	1861-1867

Lieutenant Governors of the Province of Quebec

Sir Narcisse-Fortunat Belleau (1808-1894)	1867-1873
René-Édouard Caron (1821-1876)	1873-1876
Luc Letellier de Saint-Just (1820-1881)	1876-1879
Théodore Robitaille (1834-1897)	1879-1884
Louis-François Rodrigue Masson (1833-1903)	1884-1887
Sir Auguste-Réal Angers (1838-1919)	1887-1892
Sir Joseph-Adolphe Chapleau (1840-1898)	1892-1898
Sir Louis-Amable Jetté (1836-1920)	1898-1908
Sir Charles-Alphonse-Pantaléon Pelletier (1837-1911)	1908-1911
Sir François-Charles-Stanislaus Langelier (1838-1915)	1911-1915
Sir Pierre-Laurent-Damase-Évariste Leblanc (1853-1918)	1915-1918
Sir Charles Fitzpatrick (1853-1942)	1918-1923
Louis-Philippe Brodeur (1862-1924)	1923-1924
Narcisse Pérodeau (1851-1932)	1924-1928
Sir Jean Lomer Gouin (1861-1929)	1928-1929
Henry George Carroll (1865-1939)	1929-1934
Esioff-Léon Patenaude (1875-1963)	1934-1939
Sir Eugène Fiset (1874-1951)	1939-1950
Gaspard Fauteux (1898-1963)	1950-1958
J.-Onésime Gagnon (1888-1961)	1958-1961
Paul Comtois (1895-1966)	1961-1966
Hugues Lapointe (1911-1983)	1966-1978
Jean-Pierre Côté (1926-	1978-1984
Gilles Lamontagne (1919-	1984

PART THREE

The Atlantic Provinces

Newfoundland
Nova Scotia
New Brunswick
Prince Edward Island

*G*overnment House, St John's: the
North Front and Porch. Photograph
1983.

Newfoundland

The oldest of all British overseas possessions, and, as an island, always a place apart, Newfoundland[1] differs perceptibly from the other Atlantic colonies in the mode of her development. At the outset the purpose of rule was to guard the fisheries, and colonization was discouraged if not forbidden.

Following centuries of European landings on her shores — by the Norsemen, by Cabot and the Bristol merchants, by the French, the Spanish, the Portuguese and the Basques — Sir Humphrey Gilbert took possession of the island in 1583 in the name of Elizabeth I of England. Struggles with the French, who had a foothold at Placentia, occupied a good part of the seventeenth century but were brought to a temporary halt in 1713 by the Treaty of Utrecht which recognized British sovereignty. The Royal Navy was called upon to keep law and order and by 1729 a naval governor was appointed for each fishing season. The first governor and commander-in-chief, Henry Osborne, headed a procession of thirty-seven of his kind before 1815, each holding office for a season or two. During the Seven Years War the French seized the capital, St John's, but by the Treaty of Paris in 1763 they relinquished all territory save two small islands off the Burin peninsula, Saint-Pierre and Miquelon. The coast of Labrador became attached to Newfoundland.

Conflict with France broke out again during the war of the American Revolution and ended with the second Treaty of Paris in 1815. Even so the treaty rights by which the French fishing fleets cured cod on the "French shore" lasted until they were formally resigned nearly a century later.

Meanwhile, against all odds, settlements had been established by the fishermen in the outports and the merchant community in St John's. The population grew to thirteen thousand by 1763 and to twenty thousand by 1804. This increase caused the governors to leave their ships and live on dry land during the summer months. Their numbers had included such sea-dogs as Fitzroy Henry Lee, who was a natural grandson of Charles II by the Duchess of Cleveland, and who is said to have been the model for Commodore Trunnion in Smollett's *Peregrine Pickle*. Among others were the charming rogue Lord Muskerry who had fought for Bonnie Prince Charlie before serving the Hanoverians; the young Sir George (later Lord) Rodney, who was to be the hero of the Battle of the Saints in 1782; and Commodore (later Admiral) John Byron, the "Foul Weather Jack" who had survived the wreck of *Wager* in 1741, and of whom his poet grandson wrote, "He had no peace at sea, nor I on land".

One of the best governors was Sir Hugh Palliser, who engaged his friend Captain James Cook to survey the Newfoundland waters. In 1766, on the anniversary of George III's coronation, their mutual friend the young botanist Joseph (later Sir Joseph) Banks was invited to a dance in St John's. Banks, noting in his diary that ladies were so scarce in the capital that the governor included his washerwoman and her sister among his guests, marvelled "that after Dancing we were conducted to a realy [sic] Elegant Supper Set out with all kinds of Wines and Italian Liqueurs To the Great Emolument of the Ladies".[2]

The first summer residence of a governor at St John's appears to have been an oak-framed house in Duke of York Street, on the property of one John Stripling, a publican.[3] It stood in its garden near the present Cochrane Street and was presumably destroyed in the great fire of 1892. It seems to have been occupied by Rear-Admiral Richard Edwards in 1779.

In that same year, however, Edwards, realizing that the city was only too open to attack in wartime,

Sir Joshua Reynolds: John Byron, 1759.

Anonymous: Fort Townshend, St John's. Drawing, 1831.

engaged a Royal Artillery lieutenant, John Thomas Caddy,* to design a house for him within the newly completed Fort Townshend. This first Government House, which formed one side of the barracks square, was finished in 1781.[4] To judge from a drawing of it showing additions made in 1812,[5] it was a low two-storeyed, slate-roofed frame building, its shape resembling that of the New England "salt-box" house, in which one slope of the roof swept down over an extended lower storey. Flanking the door were two pavilions (added in 1812) containing an entrance hall and the secretary's and clerk's offices. A report on this house by the Royal Engineers in 1825 lists its meagre amenities:

> Government House is a wooden building of two storeys, with Cellars and Offices attached, also a Stable, Cow House and Privies. It contains one Parlour, one Drawing Room, one Dining Room, and one office for the Governor, four Bed Rooms and three Servants ditto, adjoining is an Office for the Secretary and one for the Clerks.[6]

Here successive governors, including Admiral John Holloway and Sir John Duckworth, lived in the

Father of the topographical artist John Herbert Caddy (1801-1883) of Quebec and Hamilton.

summers of the first quarter of the nineteenth century.

By 1817, when the island's population was upwards of fifty thousand, civil government had developed to such an extent as to induce the governor of the day, the hard-working Sir Francis Pickmore, to spend the winter in residence at Fort Townshend. During a severe storm in February 1817 he reported to the King that the snow came into the bedrooms through every crack.[6a] So intense was the cold inside the house that he caught a chill and died of pneumonia. His corpse pickled in rum was taken home by ship after several hundred men had cut a channel through the harbour ice.

It was no wonder that in 1823 his successor Admiral Sir Charles Hamilton, who with his first wife (the painter of Beothuk Indians) had survived two winters in the house, could report, "There can be no doubt [of] the unfit state of Government House and the total want of all the usual comforts which the inhabitants of St. John's find necessary in the winter".[7] Another report, by the Royal Engineers, amplified this statement: "Government House is a very old building, in a very exposed situation. The rooms are small and by no means is it a comfortable building". It goes on to mention the "disjointed character of the house, its long dark passages and the disintegrating roof — in sum the folly of attempting to repair it".[8] One puzzles in vain over another part of the same report which states that the house could still be fitted out as a comfortable residence for the governor. In any case, abandoned in the 1830s, it was pulled down after a short period of use as a garrison hospital.

Meanwhile settlement on the island had grown, and with it the importance of the hilly capital city. But St John's was hardly prepared for the grandeur in store for it in the mind of the governor who arrived in 1825. Sir Thomas Cochrane was nothing if not grand. He was the son of Sir Alexander Cochrane, commander of

After W.R. Best: Government House, St John's, Newfoundland: *the South Front. Lithograph by W. Spreat.*

49

the Atlantic Squadron based in Bermuda, who was described by a fellow admiral as a "crack-headed, unsafe man, wrong-headed, violent and proud".[9] The son* upheld the reputation of the "mad Cochranes": proud and wilful enough, though also, as his letters reveal, a man of cultivation and political awareness who summoned the first elected Assembly in Newfoundland and instituted reforms in the administration.

In England, before departing for Newfoundland, he had made a rough plan, probably inspired in a general way by that of Admiralty House in Plymouth,

He was also a grandson of the bankrupt Earl of Dundonald.

for what was a very large house indeed for St John's. A site of twenty acres was chosen on a ridge of the Barren between Fort Townshend and Fort William, where the governor might be safe from the fires that periodically devastated the lower town. A new road (Cochrane Street) was cut from the site straight downhill into town.

The exterior design of Cochrane's house was a stripped-down version of the Italianate phase of the late Regency style in England, so that the finished building was a plain barracks-like affair of two storeys. The walls were of rough red sandstone quarried on Signal Hill, with quoins and window trim of Portland stone from England. The timbers came from Halifax. A central block projects from two large flanking wings.

The immediate reaction to Cochrane's plan came from the Royal Engineers who were charged with executing them. Their commanding officer quite rightly complained that "The plans furnished by His Excellency are very defective in detail and if they had been made by a professional man the errors in question would not have happened".[10] But they were obliged to follow them as best they could. Construction began in 1827, when twenty-eight masons, twenty-five carpenters and a slater arrived from Scotland accompanied by their wives and children;[11] they were paid at the rate of 45s.4d. a day. There was also a Scottish clerk of works.

During construction the capricious amateur architect changed his mind several times, altering the size of the wings and rearranging the interior so that chimneys already in place had to be pulled down and rebuilt. A rectangular porch was substituted for a semicircular one of Adam inspiration which would have relieved the severity of the north front.[12] Several successive Engineer officers in charge were overcome with exasperation and departed one after another. Belatedly Whitehall became aware that there had been no detailed plans on which to base the estimates of cost.[13]

In spite of all, the house was completed in June 1831 and Cochrane moved in with his family and eight servants. Shortly afterwards the roof blew off in a gale, and local builders were hired to replace it. By the time everything was in place the cost had increased fourfold from the £9000 of the original estimates.

The interior was in sharp contrast to the exterior. The lofty rooms on the ground floor, with their handsome cornices and carved marble fireplaces, their

Government House, St John's: the South Front. Photograph 1983.

Government House, St John's: the Cupola in the Central Hall. Photograph 1983.

arches into the wings with reeded frames, and their mahogany doors and papered walls, were as handsome and well proportioned as in many a Regency house in England. The central hall, originally paved with flagstones and adorned with two large Ionic columns and a niche in the wall facing the door, rose through an oval opening in the upper floor to a high iron-framed cupola at the top of the house. Corridors extended the full length of each floor. Off these, on the north side of the ground floor, were the principal rooms: the large drawing room and dining room, a second drawing room (the present ballroom) and an office for the secretary (the present billiards room). On the south side were the library (now the lieutenant governor's study), a billiards room (now the morning room), the original governor's room (now offices) and a records room (now domestic offices). Reached by an elegant if rather inconspicuous curving stair, the upper floor contained bedrooms and dressing rooms, with servants' quarters and two water closets in one of the wings.

The basement contained its full quota of servants' hall, butler's and housekeeper's rooms, a large kitchen, pantries, larders, scullery, stillroom, pastry room, three wine cellars, dairy, laundry and bathroom. Extending underground beyond the walls were an icehouse, beer cellar and wood, coal and ash houses. There was also an "air warmer"[14] which sent up hot air through flues under the floors. The basement windows were concealed in an area running around the house. This "moat" gave rise to the fantastic notion that it was intended to keep out snakes, creatures not known to inhabit the island. In any case it inevitably filled up with rain and snow.

The furniture — enough to fill a palace, according to Sir Richard Bonnycastle, commandant of the Engineers[15] — was ordered from London, apparently

Government House, St John's: the North Front. Photograph, nineteenth century.

turned and reeded legs and four drawers,* a rosewood occasional table* and two tables just outside the room.*

Government House, St John's: the Ballroom. Photograph 1983.

Mr O'Dea also mentions an old dining table from Fort Townshend, the parts of which today provide separate tables in the hall, entrance hall and porch.

No sooner was the house completed than Cochrane began to reap the fruits of extravagance and caprice. In England in 1831 an official enquiry was launched which fortunately for the house and for the governor dragged on until after his recall in 1834. But as in similar cases in other provinces, after the passage of time, there are grounds for gratitude to an extravagant man for a fine house into which the country could grow.

As the nineteenth century wore on, the inevitable changes were made to Government House in response to changing needs and fashions and the tastes of the occupants. The first Assembly met in 1833, and thereafter its members were regularly entertained at the governor's table. In the prosperous 1840s, succeeding the last naval governor Sir Henry Prescott, came Sir John Harvey, the hero of Stoney Creek in the War of 1812. He was a man of culture and tact, but his term was marred by the presence of a ne'er-do-well son who was arrested for theft. Later governors were a mixed bag, including the downright unpopular Sir Gaspard Le Marchant, who was hanged in effigy six weeks before his departure in 1862; the able and experienced Nova Scotian, Sir Charles Darling, who prepared the way for responsible government (achieved in 1855); and carousers like Sir Anthony Musgrave, who for his "licentious revels" was branded an "evil element in our society".[18]

It was in the time of the elderly but still active Sir Alexander Bannerman (whose wife had been Thomas

from the firm of Pringle.[16] By a miracle of survival most of it is still in the house. Its design is late Regency, a period in which Georgian lightness had given way to Neo-Classic monumentality. A list of the furnishings drawn up in 1829 included the pieces which a former lieutenant governor, the Hon. Fabian O'Dea, identifies as being presently in the house:[17]

> *In the drawing room:* a large rosewood circular centre table,* a rosewood sofa table,* fourteen rosewood chairs, a gilt chimney glass, an ormolu hanging lamp with four branches, a card table* and blue merino curtains.
>
> *In the dining room:* a Spanish mahogany table with telescope frame and massive turned and reeded legs,* two mahogany sideboards,* a side table,* two mahogany wine chests of sarcophagus shape,* twenty mahogany chairs,* a bronze hanging lamp and four brackets, a Brussels carpet and crimson curtains with gold valances.
>
> *In the ballroom:* two rosewood sofa tables.*
>
> *In the governor's room:* a mahogany writing-table with

Starred items are those still in Government House.

Carlyle's beloved) that the Prince of Wales paid his visit to St John's in July 1860, just before the tour of Canada and the United States. Two of the bedrooms, henceforth called the Prince of Wales rooms, were fitted up for the occasion with a great mahogany bed, a large pier glass and a hip bath. On the day of the arrival Bannerman stood on the Queen's Wharf "bothered terribly", according to the press, because the ship was ahead of schedule, and taking copious pinches of snuff "while thinking . . . 'Why, our windows are not washed yet.' "[19] Sunday School children sang the National Anthem in the grounds of Government House, and in the afternoon there was a levée at which the young Prince appeared in a scarlet tunic, black trousers and sash. This function was attended by "a very promiscuous crowd, lawyers, doctors, judges, soldiers, bishops, naval officers, editors, volunteers and civilians; long and short, stout and thin, of intelligent looks, of stupid looks, of humble bearing, or of manifestly quiet self-importance".[20] A grand ball in the

Government House, St John's: the Drawing Room. Photograph 1983.

Colonial Building, with "not an ugly woman in the room", was the subject of a plate in *Illustrated London News*.[21] A regatta on Quidi Vidi Lake, and the presentation of a black Newfoundland dog with an engraved silver collar, concluded the festivities. A few years later, in 1866, Newfoundland won further fame at the inauguration of the first successful cable link between America and England.

Quite by accident, in the period of Sir John Glover, the house acquired the painted ceilings that grace its principal rooms. Their elegant scrolls, Pompeian vases and garlands and other Neo-Classic motives were the work of one Alexander Pindikowsky, an itinerant Polish art teacher and scene painter who was arrested in 1880 for forging cheques. He won remission of a month and a week of a fifteen-month sentence to hard labour by carrying out decorative work in Government House and the Colonial Building.

At one time, possibly as late as Sir Henry MacCallum's period, a small outer porch was added to the main entrance for added protection from the gales. At another time a greenhouse was built on the south side of the house as a refuge from the long winters. In the wooded grounds were a porter's lodge, secretary's house, coach-house and, for entertainment, a paddock, a croquet lawn and the tennis court which Glover in the 1870s placed at the disposal of the officers from H.M. ships. The roads, lawns, gardens, orchard and kitchen garden were at one time maintained, summer and winter, by prison labour.[22]

The brief tenure of Sir Henry Blake in 1887-8 provides a charming vignette of life in Government House. In September 1887, very shortly after the family's arrival in St John's, the Governor's nine-year-old son Maurice found an old ledger in a cupboard and used its blank pages as a diary. This first literary effort of an imaginative boy who grew up into a barrister,

Government House, St John's: the Gate House. Photograph by the Author, 1976.

explorer, airman and author reflects not only the official activities of the house, including a children's fancy dress ball and a great dinner for the poor of the capital, but the life of the family: the theatricals and concerts, the games of cricket and hockey, the long walks to Signal Hill and an exciting trip to Placentia on the new railway. There were also the lessons at home under a tutor, the building of huts and engines and the care of a menagerie of pets: parrot, puppy, pony, tame seal and the goats Kiddy and Viddy. Maurice and the other children held a mock Assembly which decided in favour of Confederation with Canada.[22a]

The interiors were radically altered by Mac-Callum's purchase of Victorian dark oak Renaissance Revival furniture. These pieces, along with the baubled curtains and table covers, effectively masked the Regency lines of the rooms. The old chandeliers were replaced by gasoliers which in their turn gave way to electric lamps — 165 of them throughout the house — in the late nineteenth century. The changes and improvements were brought to a temporary halt by the great fire of 1892, in Sir Terence O'Brien's time. Money from the banks in town was brought to Government House for safekeeping, and homeless people were accommodated in tents on the Barren adjoining the grounds.

A few years later, the very Irish and rhetorical Sir Cavendish Boyle wrote the words of what became the national song, "Ode to Newfoundland". He persuaded his composer friend Sir Hubert Parry (of "Jerusalem" fame) to set it to music, and in 1902 at one of its first performances a Miss Carroll, "robed in pink, white and green, stood on a pedestal representing Terra Nova, and was supported on the one side by a fisherman bearing the 'Native' colours and on the other by a Naval Reservist supporting the Royal Standard".[23] Parry had in fact provided alternative tunes, the one "of more masculinity", the other "with more sentiment". The latter was adopted.[24]

The year 1901 saw two important events at Government House. The first, in October, was the visit of the Duke and Duchess of Cornwall and York at the conclusion of their extended Canadian tour. This visit afforded a golden opportunity to refurbish the house, the exterior of which was decorated for the occasion with giant rosettes of red, white and blue bunting. The official ball was held in the more spacious rooms of the Colonial Building. The second event, in December, was Guglielmo Marconi's transmission of the letter "S" in Morse code by wireless telegraphy from Signal Hill to Cornwall. The great Italian reported to the governor both before and after the event.

In the earlier part of the twentieth century the number of visitors increased perceptibly and the tempo of life in Government House accelerated accordingly. Though Newfoundland remained a separate Dominion (the attempts at Confederation with Canada having failed in the 1860s) a number of the governors general of Canada paid fraternal visits. It was perhaps in anticipation of the arrival of Prince Arthur, Duke of

The Duke of Connaught's Visit to Government House, St John's, 1914. Left to right: second from left, the Governor, Sir Walter Davidson; Duke of Connaught; Lady Davidson.

Connaught, in 1914 that an abortive plan was drawn up for improving the grounds of Government House with a semicircular drive and by adding a balcony and "piazza" to the house. After a State dinner and ball Connaught departed to inspect the curing of cod at Belle Isle and the work of the Grenfell Mission on the Labrador coast. The pretensions of the house at this point are reflected in the printing of dinner menus in French — though not without a few errors in spelling.[25]

The first visit of the Prince of Wales in 1919 — also the year of Alcock and Brown's first transatlantic flight from Newfoundland to England — was the occasion for a modernization of the old Prince of Wales rooms. But the house still boasted only two or three bathrooms.

The following decades were unhappy ones for Newfoundland. The economic depression of the 1930s deprived her of the finances to sustain Dominion status, so that from 1934 to 1949 the constitution was suspended and the country was governed by a commission of six functioning under two successive governors, Sir David Anderson and Sir Humphry Walwyn. In the recession that followed wartime prosperity, the movement for union with Canada was revived and hotly debated. With Joseph Smallwood as its champion, and a governor sent from England to implement it, Confederation came to pass in 1949 against heavy opposition. Feelings against the governor, Sir Gordon MacDonald, ran so high that this dour teetotaler and former coal-miner was insulted in an anonymous jingle published in a newspaper. It was an acrostic in which the initial letters of the lines spelled out "THE BASTARD".[26]

In 1949 one of the leading advocates of union, Sir Albert Walsh, was named lieutenant governor. On his resignation the same year to become the province's chief justice he was succeeded by Sir Leonard Outer-bridge under whom the transition from independent Dominion to province, and from governor to lieutenant governor, was accomplished smoothly.

To the credit of his successors the traditions and dignity of Government House have been upheld and enhanced. Campbell Macpherson, Mr Fabian O'Dea, Mr John Harnum, Mr Gordon Winter, Anthony Paddon, and the present incumbent James McGrath, have all made their contributions to the position of the Monarchy in modern Canada. Recent proposals to make the interior of the house more welcoming to the citizens of the province, and an ambitious plan to transform the grounds into a show place with formal gardens and a fountain, indicate that the old house is far from standing still. In our own day it remains a living monument to the warm attachment of Newfoundlanders to the Crown.

King George VI and Queen Elizabeth in a car at the entrance of Government House, St John's, 1939.

Governors of Newfoundland 1729-1949

Henry Osborne (1694-1771)	1729-1731
George Fiennes Clinton (c.1688-1761)	1731
Edward Falkingham (c.1683-1757)	1732
Robert MacCarthy, Viscount Muskerry of Cork and titular Earl of Cancarty	1733-1734
Fitzroy Henry Lee (1699-1750)	1735-1737
Philip Vanbrugh	1738
Henry Medley	1739
Lord George Graham (1715-1747)	1740
Thomas Smith	1741 and 1743
The Hon. John Byng (1704-1757)	1742
Sir Charles Hardy (c.1714-1780)	1744
Richard Edwards (I)	1745
Charles Watson (1714-1757)	1748-1749
George Brydges Rodney, 1st Baron Rodney (1718-1792)	1749-1752
Francis William Drake (d.1788/9)	1752-1753
Hugh Bonfoy (c.1720-1762)	1753-1754
Richard Dorrill (c.1719-1762)	1755
Richard Edwards (II) (c.1715-1795)	1757-1758 and 1779-1781
James Webb (d.1761)	1760-1761
Thomas Graves, 1st Baron Graves (1725-1802)	1761-1764
Sir Hugh Palliser, Bt (1723-1796)	1764-1768
The Hon. John Byron (1723-1786)	1769-1772
Molyneux Shuldham, 1st Baron Shuldham (c.1717-1798)	1772-1774
Robert Duff (d.1787)	1775-1776
John Montagu (1719-1795)	1776-1778
John Campbell (c.1720-1790)	1782-1786
John Elliot (d.1808)	1786-1789
Mark Milbanke (1724-1805)	1789-1792
Sir Richard King (1730-1806)	1792-1794
Sir James Wallace (1731-1803)	1794-1797
Sir William Waldegrave, 1st Lord Radstock (1753-1825)	1797-1800
Sir Charles Morice Pole, Bt (1757-1830)	1800-1801
James Gambier, 1st Lord Gambier (1756-1833)	1802-1804
Sir Erasmus Gower (1742-1814)	1804-1806
John Holloway (1742-1826)	1807-1809
Sir John Thomas Duckworth, Bt (1748-1817)	1810-1812
Sir Richard Godwin Keats (1757-1834)	1813-1816
Sir Francis Pickmore (d.1818)	1816-1818
Sir Charles Hamilton, Bt (1767-1849)	1818-1824
Sir Thomas John Cochrane (1789-1872)	1825-1834
Sir Henry Prescott (1783-1874)	1834-1841
Sir John Harvey (1778-1852)	1841-1846
Sir John Gaspard Le Marchant (1803-1874)	1847-1852
Ker Baillie Hamilton (1804-1889)	1852-1855
Sir Charles Henry Darling (1809-1870)	1855-1857
Sir Alexander Bannerman (1788-1864)	1857-1863
Sir Anthony Musgrave (1828-1888)	1864-1869
Sir Stephen John Hill (1809-1891)	1869-1875
Sir John Hawley Glover (1829-1885)	1875-1881 and 1883-1885
Sir Henry Berkeley Hardinge Maxse (1832-1883)	1881-1883
Sir George William des Voeux (1834-1909)	1886-1887
Sir Henry Arthur Blake (1848-1918)	1887-1888
Sir John Terence Nicolls O'Brien (1830-1903)	1888-1895
Sir Herbert Harley Murray (1829-1904)	1895-1898
Sir Henry Edmund MacCallum (1852-1919)	1898-1901
Sir Charles Cavendish Boyle (1849-1916)	1901-1904
Sir William MacGregor (1846-1919)	1904-1909

Sir Ralph Champneys Williams (1848-1927)	1909-1913
Sir Walter Edward Davidson (1859-1923)	1913-1917
Sir Charles Alexander Harris (1855-1947)	1917-1922
Sir William Lamond Allardyce (1861-1930)	1922-1928
Sir John Middleton (1870-1954)	1928-1932
Sir David Murray Anderson (1874-1936)	1932-1936
Sir Humphrey Thomas Walwyn (1879-1957)	1936-1946
Sir Gordon MacDonald, Baron MacDonald of Gwaenysgor (1888-1966)	1946-1949

Lieutenant Governors of the Province of Newfoundland 1949-

Sir Albert Joseph Walsh (1900-1958)	1949
Sir Leonard Cecil Outerbridge (1888-	1949-1957
Campbell Leonard Macpherson (1907-1973)	1957-1963
Fabian O'Dea (1918-	1963-1971
Ewart John Arlington Harnum (1910-	1971-1974
Gordon Arnaud Winter (1912-	1974-1981
William Anthony Paddon (1914-	1981-1986
James Aloysius McGrath (1932-	1986

*G*overnment House, Halifax: the
Garden Front. Photograph c.1970.

Nova Scotia

The province of Nova Scotia has its origins in the troubled history of Acadia in the seventeenth and eighteenth centuries. In 1621, during one of the periods of English rule, in the reign of James I (and VI of Scotland), the territory was granted to Sir William Alexander, Earl of Stirling, under the name of New Scotland, the Latin form of which was used in the charter. In 1626 Nova Scotia received her own Order of baronets and was granted her present coat of arms. Settlement was undertaken by the younger Sir William Alexander who in 1629 established small Scots colonies, one at Port-Royal and another in Cape Breton Island. These efforts were frustrated by the return of the territory to the French in 1632. The few settlers who remained were absorbed into the Acadian population. After several more changes of hands Port-Royal was captured in 1710 by Francis Nicholson, a former governor of Virginia, and its name was changed to Annapolis Royal. By the Treaty of Utrecht in 1713 the mainland passed finally to the British Crown.

The wars of the mid-eighteenth century persuaded the British to arm the new province against the French by establishing a capital at Halifax. Prior to this the governors — Nicholson, Samuel Vetch and Richard Philipps — had lived at Annapolis. Their quarters there are described by Colonel Paul Mascarene, a French Huguenot in the British army, in a letter to his daughter, written while he was administrator of the government from 1740 to 1749:

> My apartment contains four rooms, all contiguous to one another, the first something larger than our foreroom [in Boston], the floor none of the best, is covered with painted cloth. The white walls are hung in part with four large Pictures of Mr. Smibert* — a walnut chest of drawers, a mahogany table, and six pretty good chairs fill, in some measure, the remainder.

> Over the mantle piece are a dozen of arms kept clean and in good order, with other warlike accoutrements. In this Room I dine sometimes alone but often with one or more of my friends. A door opens from this into my bed-room where my field bed, four chairs, the little round table, a desk to write upon, and my cloths chest are all the furniture that adorns it. The two closetts on the side of the chimney serve, the one to keep my papers, the other to hang my cloths. In the great room one of the closetts dispos'd on the side of the chimney is made to keep my drinkables for daily use, my case of bottles and such like. The other is for a kind of pantry and at the same time for a passage to another room wherein I keep my meal, flour, fresh and salt provisions. This communicates by a door to my kitchen and is the way by which I go every morning to order my dinner and give out what provision is necessary for it. . . . I have a bell to call my servant both from my dining and bed rooms. My Domesticks are a good old honest soldyer who makes my bed, keeps my cloths and my apartment clean and attends me very diligently and faithfully, another who was my cook when your sister was here attends me in the same office, they have a boy to assist them both. . . . The morning, now especially in winter time, I generally pass att home in useful and diverting employments. I sometimes dine abroad. The afternoons I visit some of the families in our fort town, and the evenings Capn. Handfield, Lt Amherst and three or four more of our officers meet att one another's house over a game of ombre for half pence and take part att nine, when after an hour enjoy'd quietly in my own room I go to bed.[27]

These quarters were evidently in the fort. At some later time there appears to have been a separate Government House in George Street, a two-and-a-half-storey frame house which burnt down in 1833 owing to the carelessness of an orderly. The site is marked with a plaque which also identifies the house as the birthplace of Sir Henry Darling, governor of Newfoundland.[28]

*John Smibert, the Boston painter.

It was the fourth governor of Nova Scotia after 1713, Edward Cornwallis, the twin brother of the Archbishop of Canterbury, who was charged with the founding of the new capital at Halifax. In June 1749 he arrived there with some two thousand five hundred settlers and laid out the town. Besides importing from New England the prefabricated frame of St Paul's Church, he built the first governor's house[29] on the site of the present Province House. This one-storey temporary building was occupied by Cornwallis and the two governors who succeeded him: Peregrine Hopson and Charles Lawrence (who expelled the Acadians and summoned the first Assembly).

After a scant decade of use the house was replaced under Lawrence by a permanent house on the same site. Its appearance is known to us from one of Richard Short's engraved views of Halifax drawn in 1759 and first published in 1761. It was a two-storeyed wooden house with hipped roof and dormers, a building of the ample proportions and simple design that are associated with American Georgian architecture. It was painted to simulate stone, and its only adornment was a plain porch. This second Government House was lived in for half a century comfortably enough, it would seem, by ten governors. One of these, Lord William Campbell, made additions to it

After Richard Short: Governor's House . . . Halifax, *1759. Engraved by F.A. Aveline and published by John Boydell, 1761.*

during his term from 1766 to 1773. The easy-going John Parr, governor during the arrival of the Loyalists in the 1780s, seems to have neglected it while enjoying it to the full:

> I have found everything here to exceed my expectation, have met with the greatest civility from all Ranks of People, a most excellent house and Garden, a small farm close to the Town another 70 or 80 acres at the distance of two Miles, where I propose passing two or three months in Summer a snugg little farm house upon it, a beautiful prospect, with good fishing, plenty of Provisions of all sorts except Flower, with a very good French Cook to dress them, a Cellar well stock'd with Port, Claret, Madeira, Rum, Brandy, Bowood Strong Beer, &c., a neat income (including a Regmt of Provincials of which I am Colonel) of £2200 Sterg p annum, an income far beyond my expectations, plenty of Coals and Wood against the severity of the Winter, a house well furnish'd, and warm Cloths, that upon the whole my Dear Grey, your friend Parr is as happy and comfortably seated, as you could wish an old friend to be.[30]

It is not clear from the above whether the cellar was attached to Government House or only to the farm; possibly it served both. The diarist William Dyott, on his arrival at Halifax as a young lieutenant in 1787, while Parr was still governor, noted that both the governor and the commander of the dockyard lived in "very good houses".[31] Dyott also records the first of a good many entertainments for the young Prince William Henry who was in Halifax the same year:

> In the evening a ball at the Governor's. We went about seven; his Royal Highness came about half after, and almost immediately began country dances with Miss Parr, the Governor's daughter. We changed partners every dance; he danced with all the pretty women in the room, and was just as affable as any other man.
> He did me the honour to talk a great deal to me before supper during the dance. We went to supper about twelve, a most elegant thing, nearly sixty people sat

> down. . . . After supper he gave five or six bumper toasts. . . . We had a most jolly evening, and he retired about two o'clock.[32]

The last dance of the evening was usually a strenuous one called the "Country Bumpkin", which lasted nearly an hour. Dyott and the lively Prince became bosom friends for the rest of the visit.

When that much grander man than Parr, the charming if overbearing John Wentworth, arrived in 1792 as governor, complaints were heard of the unfitness of Government House. Wentworth, the former Royal Governor of New Hampshire, his native province, had spent some years in England after the Revolution and from his family connection with the Marquess of Rockingham knew well the life of a great country house. According to him, Government House in Halifax had been built "chiefly of green wood . . . and the larger timbers generally rotten"; the whole house was in fact "in Danger of falling into the Cellar".[33] But his chief reason for pressing so hard for a new house was obviously his desire for a mansion fitting to his position and that of his beautiful wife Frances.

In the meantime, in order to escape discomfort, he lived for a time in his own house, Prince's Lodge, on Bedford Basin, which had been leased to Prince Edward, Duke of Kent, and which the Prince had vacated when he and Julie de Saint-Laurent left Halifax in 1800. Yet in old Government House he was obliged to entertain several royal visitors: not only the Duke of Kent in 1794 and 1799 but three French princes, Louis-Philippe (then Duke of Orléans and later King of France) and his two brothers, who at this time of war with France were technically prisoners on parole.

In those days of "irresponsible" government Wentworth felt free to press relentlessly towards his goal. In 1796 he persuaded the Assembly to vote £600 for plans, estimates and land, and the following year to

Attributed to John Singleton Copley: Sir John Wentworth, Bt, 1791.

John Singleton Copley: Lady Wentworth, 1769.

pass an enabling act. Construction began in 1798. The architect was Isaac Hildrith[34] (1741-1807), a master builder and surveyor from Yorkshire, who had gone to Norfolk, Virginia, and had lived at Charleston, South Carolina, until its evacuation, and subsequently in Jamaica and New York before fleeing as a Loyalist to Shelburne in 1789. He had moved to Halifax where he was employed in surveying the proposed canals in the province. Hildrith had been back and forth to England several times and knew the Regency style in architecture. Wentworth, for his part, had also been in England during the building of Wentworth House, his kinsman and protector Lord Rockingham's seat in Yorkshire. Its

architect had been the greatest designer of the period, Robert Adam. The Governor had also the advantage of knowing American building methods and materials from his years as surveyor general of America.

The distinguished design of the new Government House was thus far from being the work of an amateur or a provincial builder. By long-standing tradition it came from the brothers Adam.[35] Though this is unlikely, the available evidence points to Hildrith's having had access, through Wentworth or the commissioner of construction Michael Wallace, to a book of designs[36] published in 1795 by George Richardson, an assistant in Robert Adam's London office. Sir John

Summerson, the present-day authority on the architecture of the period, has noted the close relation of the Halifax design to two of the plates in Richardson's book.[37] The rusticated basement, the closed arches over the windows and the ashlar masonry of the upper storey articulated on the garden front with pilasters — all are features of the Richardson designs, as are the curved bays and the small-scale Classic detail in the cornices.

The building materials used in Government House came mostly from Nova Scotia: stone from Lunenburg, Pictou County (red sandstone), Antigonish and Cape Breton. But there were also English bricks, Scottish roofing slates and South American mahogany for the interior doors.

The site was one originally chosen for Province House, in the "south suburbs" of the Halifax of that day; by today's standards it is close to the present Province House. But the new site, between Pleasant (now Barrington) Street and Hollis Street, had the advantage of allowing Government House to assume the aspect of an English country seat, with a road front on the west and a garden front on the east overlooking the harbour. The only drawback is that the road front is a little lower than the present street level, so that the house loses something of its impact. But the symmetrical three-storeyed façade on this side is handsome with its columned porch and the two-storey circular-ended wings at each end projecting considerably from the central block of the building.

Construction began in 1798 and proceeded slowly. Only in September 1800, just after the departure of the Duke of Kent, was the cornerstone laid. This was done with much ceremony.[38] Wentworth took the leading part, in the presence of an admiral, a general, the colonels of the regiments stationed in Halifax, the Bench and members of the Assembly. The procession wound from the old Government House to the new headed by a band playing "God Save the King", "Rule

John Woolford: Government House (Halifax) from the S.W. *Aquatint and Etching, 1819.*

John Woolford: Government House (Halifax) from the N.E. *Aquatint and Etching, 1819.*

Britannia" and other "appropriate airs". After speeches had been made, the Revd Robert Stanser, rector of St Paul's, read prayers and pronounced the house to be a "Monument of the increasing Prosperity of this infant Colony". The workmen were treated to food and drink.

Government House, Halifax: the Hall. Photograph 1982.

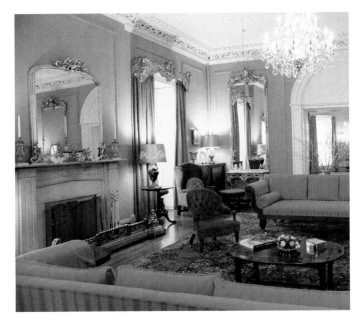

Government House, Halifax: the Drawing Room. Photograph 1982.

The interior plan of the house was simple, the proportions of the rooms noble. Off the central hall with its paired Ionic columns and Palladian doorway at its east end were the morning room (now hung with Oriental foil paper painted with cherry blossom), the pantry and the governor's office and waiting rooms. The south wing was entirely taken up by the drawing room and dining room, the north wing by the columned levée room (or ballroom) with its fine cornices and white marble fireplaces. From a second hall rose a splendid circular-ended stair with delicately carved balusters. Upstairs were the large principal bedrooms facing the harbour, guest rooms and a nursery. The basement, with stone floor and massive partitions intended to halt the spread of fire, contained the kitchens and other domestic offices.

The interior architecture is said to have been the work of John Merrick (d. 1829), the architect of Province House.[39] In the great bedroom overlooking the harbour is what is described in a document of 1804 as a "statuary Marble Chimney Piece sunk pannels in frieze & pilasters carved paterns in blockings, Figure in Tablet & Statuary".[40] It is signed by the London sculptor Richard Westmacott, whose brother John, an army officer, was murdered in Halifax; this relationship may have led to the commission. There are other fine marble fireplaces throughout the house. Restrained Classic detail, worthy of contemporary work in England, is to be found in all the mouldings, cornices and capitals. The original paint colours included two Regency favourites, olive and lemon.

The grounds of Government House included not only the gardens facing Hollis Street but a property across Barrington Street, adjoining the Old Churchyard. This plot contained stables, wash house, fowl house, coal house, a garden hut and an icehouse.

*Government House, Halifax: the
Ballroom. Photograph 1982.*

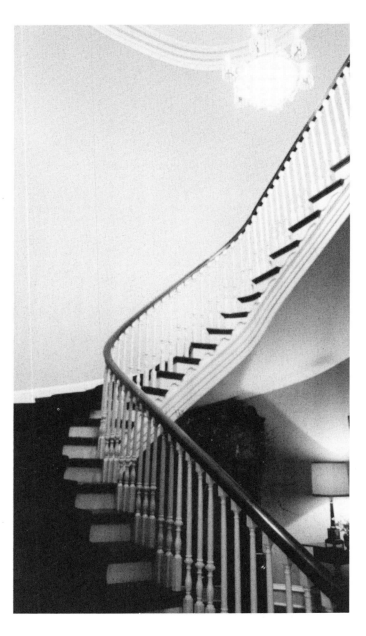

Government House, Halifax: the Stair. Photograph 1982.

Sir John* and Lady Wentworth (whom Dyott had earlier described as "rather more partial to our sex than to her own" and as sharing a "mutual passion" with Prince William Henry)[41] moved into the house in 1805. The move took place even before all ninety pieces of the furniture which Richard John Uniacke, commissioner for Government House, had ordered from London, arrived. Presumably in the meantime the Governor had made do with what was worth transferring from the old house. This latter, he informed the Assembly, might now be removed to make room for the "State" House.[42]

Eventually the furniture arrived. According to reports made to the Assembly after Wentworth's departure, it included the following:

> *In the levée room:* seven "Turkish Sophas", twelve cane-bottom chairs with cushions, a looking-glass, three lustres with glass tops, seven wall "branches" for candles, window cornices and draperies.
> *In the dining room:* a "set of Dining Tables" in mahogany, twenty-four mahogany chairs, a mahogany sideboard, six window curtains, draperies and cornices, and a carpet.
> *In the drawing room:* twenty-four cane-bottom chairs and covers, a mahogany commode, three mahogany tables, four armchairs, two sofas with bolsters, a looking-glass, a hanging lustre, two chimney candelabra and a Brussels carpet.
> *In the salon:* two mahogany tables, two pair tables, two blue satin sofas, twelve armchairs, two large armchairs, eighteen chairs with no arms, china ornaments, three looking-glasses, a steel register stove, chimney candlesticks and a Brussels carpet.[43]

There appears to have been but one water closet for the entire house. Over the years the original furnishings disappeared in the periodic refurbishings of the house,

He had been created Baronet in 1795.

but in recent years it has been replaced by fine period pieces, so that the present aspect of the house is much like that of the original.

As Wentworth had intended, Government House became the centre of provincial life. Thomas Chandler Haliburton, in his nostalgic novel of 1849, *The Old Judge*, describes a series of entertainments on New Year's Day as they were in early days:

> It was on the first day of January, there was a levée in the morning, a dinner party in the afternoon, and a ball in the evening. . . .
>
> The dinner was an official one; the guests were the various heads of departments in the place; and it passed off much in the same manner as similar ones elsewhere. . . .
>
> The ball to which I allude being a public one the invitations were very numerous, and embraced the military, navy, and staff, the members of the legislature, which was then in session, and all the civilians whose names were to be found on the most extended list that had been formed at the time. Having dined at the palace that day, I happened to be present at the arrivals. The guests were shown into the drawing-room, and courteously, though ceremoniously, received by the Governor, his Lady, and staff. . . .
>
> [The ballroom] was a large and handsome apartment, tastefully decorated and well-lighted; and the effect produced by the rich and various uniforms of the military and navy was gay, and even brilliant — more so, indeed, than is generally seen in a provincial town in England; for the garrison consisted of three regiments, and the greater part of the fleet upon the station was in port at the time. At the upper end of the room were the Governor, Lady Sampson,* the Admiral and his Lady, and the heads of the civil and military departments of the place and their families. Those next in rank adorned the sides of the room; and groups of those who made no pretension to that equivocal word "position" occupied and filled the lower end. . . .

> In a short time the quadrilles were formed, and all . . . appeared gay and happy. Indeed, some of the young ladies from the country danced with a vigour and energy that showed their whole hearts were engaged in displaying what they considered most valuable qualities, exertion and endurance. The effect of the sudden cessation of music in a ball-room is always ludicrous, as the noise compels people to talk louder than usual; and, when it terminates, the conversation is continued for a while in the same key. . . .
>
> The party now began to move towards the supper-room. . . . The tables were tastefully and beautifully arranged. . . . Whatever doubt there might have been as to the possibility of a ball conferring happiness, there could be none as to the enjoyment derived from the supper. In approving or partaking, nearly all seemed to join; a few claimed exemption from age, and no one objected to a *vis-à-vis*; and, if some had danced with all their hearts, an infinitely greater number ate and drank with as much relish as if eating and drinking were as unusual a thing as waltzing. . . .
>
> The last dance lasted for a long time; for the termination of every thing agreeable is always deferred to the utmost moment of time. At length the band played "God Save the King" which was the signal for parting.[44]

Meanwhile the cost of Government House had mounted to considerably more than the £10,500 voted by the Assembly. Wentworth brazened out the complaints of the legislators and had won the battle by the time of his departure in 1808. His successor Sir George Prevost, though he considered the house too grand for the Halifax of his day, maintained the trappings of state. Early in his term an unusual visitor appeared at his door. This was Aaron Burr who had been vice-president of the United States under Jefferson. He appeared in the spring of 1808 under the assumed name of Edwards. His purposes were to propose a joint

After Robert Field: Sir George Prevost, Bt. Copy of the portrait of 1808 in the Séminaire de Québec.

**A fictitious name for the Governor's wife.*

Anglo-American hegemony in Spanish America for the security of the infant republic and generally to set out the Federalist case for reconciliation between the United States and Britain. All of this came to nothing when Madison's Democrats declared war on Britain in 1812.

Six years later, towards the end of the War of 1812, the succeeding governor Sir John Sherbrooke received another mysterious American visitor. This time it was an emissary of Caleb Strong, governor of Massachusetts, who was under pressure to defy the American government and make a separate peace which would end the hardships imposed on New England by the war, and to sound out British willingness to help in case New England seceded from the union. The emissary, probably one George Herbert

G.H. Andrews: Reception at Government House, Halifax, August 1st, 1860. *Water colour, 1860.*

of Maine, put his suggestions down on paper and Sherbrooke forwarded them to Whitehall.[45] Any further development of the matter became unnecessary when peace terms were signed in December 1814.

In 1840 Lord Sydenham, Governor General of British North America, visited Halifax and at Government House heard Joseph Howe plead the case for responsible government in Nova Scotia. The two, it is recorded, parted "in mutual confidence and respect".[46] Responsible government was achieved eight years later when Sir John Harvey swore in the Reform cabinet in Government House. Howe became provincial secretary and as such was the Governor's chief adviser.

By this time the life of the house was running along well worn tracks. There were the annual garden parties, the levées ablaze with candles and the frequent dinners for members of the Assembly. But there were also the inevitable changes in the house and grounds. These were mercifully spared from the proposal of one leader of the government in 1852 that the house should be turned into a lunatic asylum; he was perhaps reacting to the extravagance of the governor of the day, Sir Gaspard Le Marchant. Two years later, a fire in the roof caused serious damage to the attics and to the ceilings, cornices and floors of the first floor; the repairs cost £2000.

The great event of the middle years of the nineteenth century was the visit of the Prince of Wales in 1860, in Lord Mulgrave's time. In preparation for this, the drawing room and dining room in the west wing underwent a complete redecoration. Regency cornices were replaced with elaborate openwork Victorian ones. Gilt console tables were placed below large mirrors with Rococo Revival frames; the window cornices bore the Prince of Wales's feathers.[47] For the young Prince a State dinner was held for forty-six guests. The drawing room appears in a sparkling water colour of the Prince's levée. The artist was George

Government House, Halifax. Photograph c.1865.

Henry Andrews (1816-1898) who accompanied the tour; and wood engravings of this and other subjects were published in *Illustrated London News*.[48] The decorations of 1860 remain in place today. Out of doors, a guard of honour stood under festooned arches over the gates, which were illuminated by night.

From later in the century come titbits of information about further changes in the house. The chandeliers were fitted for gas in 1850. During the American Civil War a Southern ship took refuge in Halifax harbour and after some soul-searching its captain was received by the governor. In 1864 a charwoman's services were to be obtained for ninety cents a day. In 1868 there was an expenditure for stopping rat holes in the house. A summerhouse was in place in the garden by 1878, as were the iron gates in Barrington Street. And by the eighties a variety of Victorian furnishings had been purchased, including chairs covered in plush and velvet, stuffed sofas, a whatnot and white lace curtains. A telephone was installed in 1881. Also in the eighties, Archibald McLelan's wife kept a Jersey cow in the grounds, but, failing to persuade the cook to churn the butter, was

A Garden Party in Government House Grounds, Halifax. Photograph c.1925-30.

Government House.

Garden party on Government House grounds (east side) during term of office of Lieut.-Gov. J. C. Tory (1925-31)

obliged to perform the task herself. In 1890 Sir Malachy Daly's goods and library were auctioned off in Government House after his death.

Six years after Nova Scotia's agonized entry into Confederation the leading opponent of union, Joseph Howe, himself became lieutenant governor. Unfortunately the veteran politician died a few weeks after his installation, but legend has it that his ghost may still be seen treading the stair into the garden. In 1874 the house was again threatened when another premier advocated selling it for use as a hotel. The failure of this move was providential, as in the last quarter of the century the important visitors to Halifax became more numerous. When the young Prince Arthur, Queen Victoria's third son and a future governor general of Canada, arrived in 1869, a round of picnics, regattas and moose hunts was organized in his honour. The lieutenant governor of that day, Sir Hastings Doyle,* is

*A relative of the Sir Francis Doyle of "The Private of the Buffs".

said to have been more interested in his social and military duties and the artistry of his French cook than in Nova Scotia politics at the critical period of repeal agitation.

Successive governors general of Canada came to Government House in spite of the feeling against Confederation. In 1873, in Sir Adams Archibald's time, Lord and Lady Dufferin stayed aboard their ship in harbour but were accorded a "drawing-room" and a dinner in the house. Lady Dufferin, always quick to see the comic side of life, tells in her diary of the playing of "God Save the Queen" at dinner. After the first stanza everyone sat down but the band continued to play verse after verse to the accompaniment of several more ups and downs. The Dufferins' sendoff included a torchlight procession with fire engines.[49]

In 1878 a new governor general, Lord Lorne, landed at Halifax on his way to Ottawa. He and his wife Princess Louise were met on board their ship by her younger brother Prince Alfred, who was then in Halifax as a naval officer, and were greeted offically at the landing stage by Sir John A. Macdonald, "pale but erect" after a monumental drinking bout.[50] The Princess too was pale but beautiful after the voyage and only picked at her dinner at Government House. A few years later her nephew, the sailor-prince who became King George V, called at the house when his ship was in harbour. The modest blue-eyed young man with his "boyish, bashful expression" endeared himself to Halifax; and when in 1901 he returned with his wife, as Duke and Duchess of York, the province spent $400 on flowers for the State dinner held by the lieutenant governor Alfred Jones and more than six hundred for the hire of barouches.

Lord Aberdeen, governor general from 1893 to 1898, came several times. His energetic wife used these visits to organize the Local Council of Women. On one occasion she observed that at a garden party at

Government House "everything was as well done as they could be in London", and on another that "everything is so smart & proper we have to be on our Ps and Qs".[51]

In the new century the procession of royal visitors accelerated. Another sailor-prince, Albert, who became King George VI, stayed in the house in 1913. His elder brother, Edward, Prince of Wales, paid his first visit in

Government House, Halifax, 1976: The Queen with the Lieutenant Governor of Nova Scotia, the Honourable Clarence Gosse.

1919. At a ball in his honour he enhanced his position as the idol of the younger generation by requesting a popular dance tune of the day, "Oh how I hate to get up in the morning". King George VI and Queen Elizabeth stayed at Government House at the end of their triumphal tour of Canada in 1939. The present Sovereign and Prince Philip have been in residence a number of times. It was in 1959 that the Queen presided over a meeting of John Diefenbaker's cabinet held round the dining-room table and approved the nomination of General Georges-P. Vanier as governor general.

The two World Wars, which scarred the face of Halifax, left Government House untouched. It escaped both the explosion of 1917 and the riots of 1945, as it did the protests of Hungarian refugees when the Soviet First Deputy Premier stayed there in 1959 on his way to Mexico.

Recent lieutenant governors (who have included such prominent Nova Scotians as J.A.D. McCurdy, the pioneer of aviation) have demonstrated their pride in the old house not only by maintaining it to a high standard of operation but by restoring it sensitively and adding fine furnishings. Occupied today by Their Honours Lloyd R. Crouse and his wife, it stands as a lasting monument to the affection of Nova Scotians for the Crown and for their historic province.

Queen Elizabeth The Queen Mother, with John Shaffner, Lieutenant Governor, at the entrance of Government House, Halifax, 1979

The Prince and Princess of Wales leaving Government House, Halifax, 1983.

H.M. The Queen and Prince Philip, with the Prime Minister, John G. Diefenbaker (left) and his Cabinet, in Government House, Halifax, 1959.

Governors and Lieutenant Governors of Nova Scotia 1712-1867

Francis Nicholson (1655-1728)	1712-1715
Samuel Vetch (1668-1732)	1715-1717
Richard Philipps (c.1661-1750)	1717-1749
The Hon. Edward Cornwallis (1712/3-1776)	1749-1752
Peregrine Thomas Hopson (d.1759)	1752-1755
Charles Lawrence (c.1709-1760)	1753-1760
Henry Ellis (1721-1806) (never entered into office)	1761-1763
Jonathan Belcher (1710-1776)	1761-1763
Montagu Wilmot (d.1766)	1763-1766
Michael Francklin (1733-1782)	1766
Lord William Campbell (c.1730-1778)	1766-1773
Francis Legge (c.1719-1783)	1773-(1782)
Mariot Arbuthnot (1711-1794)	1776-1778
Sir Richard Hughes, Bt (1729?-1812)	1778-1781
Sir Andrew Snape Hamond, Bt (1738-1828)	1781-1782
John Parr (1725-1791)	1782-1791
Sir John Wentworth, Bt (1737-1820)	1792-1808
Sir George Prevost (1767-1816)	1808-1811
Sir John Coape Sherbrooke (1764-1830)	1811-1816
George Ramsay, 9th Earl of Dalhousie (1770-1838)	1816-1820
Sir James Kempt (1764-1854)	1820-1828
Sir Peregrine Maitland (1777-1854)	1828-1834
Sir Colin Campbell (1776-1847)	1834-1840
Lucius Bentinck Cary, 10th Viscount Falkland (1803-1884)	1840-1846
Sir John Harvey (1778-1852)	1846-1852
Sir John Gaspard Le Marchant (1803-1874)	1852-1858
George Augustus Constantine Phips, 3rd Earl of Mulgrave, later Marquess of Normanby (1819-1890)	1858-1863
Sir Richard Graves MacDonnell (1814-1881)	1864-1865
Sir William Fenwick Williams, Bt (1800-1883)	1865-1867

Lieutenant Governors of the Province of Nova Scotia 1867-

Sir Charles Hastings Doyle (1804-1883)	1867-1873
Joseph Howe (1804-1873)	1873
Sir Adams George Archibald (1814-1892)	1873-1883
Matthew Henry Richey (1828-1911)	1883-1888
Archibald Woodbury McLelan (1824-1890)	1888-1890
Sir Malachy Bowes Daly (1836-1920)	1890-1900
Alfred Gilpin Jones (1824-1906)	1900-1906
Duncan Cameron Fraser (1845-1910)	1906-1910
James Drummond McGregor (1838-1918)	1910-1915
David McKeen (1839-1916)	1915-1916
MacCallum Grant (1845-1928)	1916-1925
James Robson Douglas (1876-1934)	1925
James Cranswick Tory (1862-1944)	1925-1930
Frank Stanfield (1872-1931)	1930-1931
Walter Harold Covert (1865-1949)	1931-1937
Robert Irwin (1865-1941)	1937-1940
Frederick Francis Mathers (1871-1947)	1940-1942
Henry Ernest Kendall (1864-1949)	1942-1947
John Alexander Douglas McCurdy (1886-1961)	1947-1952
Alistair Fraser (1885-1964)	1952-1958
Ernest Chester Plow (1904-	1958-1963
Henry Poole McKeen (1892-	1963-1968
Victor de Bedia Oland (1913-1983)	1968-1973
Clarence L. Gosse (1912-	1973-1978
John Elvin Shaffner (1911-	1978-1984
Alan Rockwell Abraham (1931-	1984-1989
Lloyd R. Crouse (1918-	1989

*C*aptain I. Campbell: "Indian Dance" at Government House, Fredericton, on the 1st of January 1835. *Water colour, 1835.*

New Brunswick

The territory that was to form New Brunswick became a part of British North America during the Seven Years War. In 1758, after the fall of Louisbourg, Robert Monckton laid waste the Acadian settlements on the St John River, and in 1763 after the Treaty of Paris these lands were annexed to Nova Scotia. It was the Loyalist influx after the American Revolution, replacing the deported Acadians, that led to the formation of a new province. The American war officially ended in 1783 and by the following year there were already enough inhabitants to justify separation from Nova Scotia. In spite of the existence of Saint John, near the site of the old French Fort La Tour, the village of Fredericton further up the St John River was chosen as capital because of its safety from attack by sea. The first governor of New Brunswick was Thomas Carleton, brother of, and former quartermaster general to, Sir Guy Carleton, governor of Quebec.

In 1785 Thomas Carleton chose a picturesque site beside the river, at a little remove from the town, and here two years later he built his house. The plot of land was near the site of an old French mission and an old Indian burying-ground. The house, which was to become the first Government House of the province, was built in a style roughly similar to that of the second house at Halifax: the American wooden Georgian. It was, however, on a somewhat smaller scale and had a gambrel roof and (at one time) a railed-in "widow's walk" at its summit. Its two storeys were separated by a string-course in wood, and the door had a fanlight and sidelights. At some later date it acquired a pediment, as well as lateral wings and small pavilions, additions which lent it something of the aspect of the first Spencer Wood at Quebec at the stage when the latter house was transformed into a rustic villa by the incorporation of outbuildings. In the grounds at Fredericton were the usual porter's lodge and other smaller structures including a buttery.

As soon as it was finished, Carleton's house became the scene of all the established activities of a colonial governor's palace: the dinners, balls, levées and card parties. Added to these were the winter pastimes of a cold climate, the skating and the sleighing. A ball which the Carletons held in 1795 is fulsomely described in a contemporary newspaper account:

> The ladies were of the best families only, but the gentlemen were of all sorts. . . . Governor Carleton was unusually animated through the whole evening, and by his affability diffused a general ease and gaiety through the whole company. Mrs. Carleton was also in high spirits. Her engaging attention and smiling courtesies were highly pleasing to her loyal visitants and added much to the happiness and hilarity of the evening. . . . The dancing continued until twelve o'clock, when the company were conducted to the banqueting room to partake of a sumptuous repast, as remarkable for its elegance as for the great rarity and delicacy of the viands. Mrs. Carleton appeared in an elegant gown of tea-coloured satin, with a white satin petticoat trimmed in shades of embroidered silk, her hair dressed in light curls and ornamented with a pearl pin with a white satin bandeau with "Vive le Roi" elegantly embroidered on it, and fastened with a brilliant button. On the right side, ostrich and peacock feathers blended. She had a large and handsome bouquet.[52]

By 1816 the provincial Assembly was ready to purchase the house as its official "place" for the governor. Carleton was now in the last of his thirty-three years' tenure of office, having long since been reduced from governor to lieutenant governor under the governor general of British North America. At the time of the purchase the property consisted of the house, its outbuildings and fifty-six acres of land running down to the river's edge.

Attributed to Sampson Towgood Roche: General Thomas Carleton. Miniature on ivory, c.1795.

80

John Woolford: First Government House, Fredericton. Wash drawing.

Anonymous: Residence of Thomas Carleton, First Governor of New Brunswick. *Drawing c.1825.*

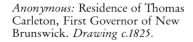

In spite of the repairs made to it in 1816 the house was in a "decayed condition" by 1820.[53] The governors of this period were expected to furnish it themselves, and Carleton's successor George Stracey Smyth was denied a request to the Assembly for furniture for the public rooms.

Smyth and his family were amateur artists and musicians. In 1822 the Governor wrote to his brother, a clergyman in England, for an "apparatus for painting", a small piano and a "tenor fiddle", along with the music of the oratorios of Handel and Haydn. Some of this was for his daughter, but his major purchase, a small organ "voiced for a church", represented his own interest. The specifications of this instrument, made by the firm founded by "Father" Smith in the seventeenth century, comprised open and stopped diapasons, principal, twelfth and fifteenth, sesquialtera and oboe; and it had a pedal-board. It arrived in Fredericton in 1822 and was installed in Government House pending the building of a proper gallery in St Ann's Church. Smyth had already sold a smaller organ to the church and now proposed to pay the difference between the new and the old and take the old one for himself.[54]

In 1824 Smyth was succeeded by a lieutenant governor important in the early development of the province. Zealous for its welfare, Sir Howard Douglas built roads and founded banks and the college which developed into the University of New Brunswick. On his arrival he tactfully chose to live in a rented house in Saint John,[55] thus appeasing the inhabitants of that city with whom the choice of Fredericton still rankled. Both there and in the capital he consolidated his position by frequently entertaining not only the government officials and leading clergy but members of the first families, the Hazens, Blisses and Chipmans. Such was his popularity that the Assembly were only too glad to buy furniture for Government House from London and from the Saint John cabinetmaker Thomas Nisbet.[56]

The visitors' books of Government House in Douglas's time[57] record many visits between 1824 and 1826 from Major John Elliott Woolford (1778-1866), barrackmaster-general at Fredericton and a relative by marriage of Lady Douglas. Woolford, a draughtsman and artist possibly trained by Paul Sandby at Woolwich, had been at Dalhousie Castle as early as 1803 and had been chosen to accompany Lord Dalhousie on his

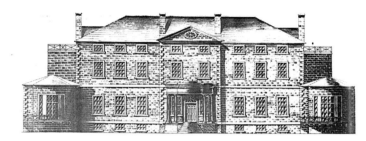

in the attics. Attached to the two-storeyed central block are one-storeyed pavilions at the four corners, with stair wells set between them at each end of the building. The pavilions on the road front have bow fronts reminiscent of Halifax. A pediment, rather small in scale for the size of the house, crowns the centre of the road front; and the river façade has a shallow bow extending the full height of the house, and a veranda running along its whole length. The entrance on the road front is lent dignity by a fine semicircular porch — an Adam touch — supported on four Doric columns. In general the design resembles that of many a Regency country house in England and Scotland, though lacking the smooth stucco surface beloved of the period.

Indoors was a columned entrance hall which ended, as at St John's, at the wall of a room on the opposite side of the house. Two staircases with finely turned balusters were placed unobtrusively at the ends of the longitudinal hall. The principal rooms were grouped on the river side and were of generous proportions. The drawing room and dining room, each thirty-six feet long, flanked a breakfast room occupying the bow. Conservatories and bathrooms were placed in the end pavilions. Fronting on the road were the offices and waiting rooms of the governor and his secretary, a council room, a small sitting room, library and music room.

On the first floor were the three principal chambers with dressing rooms attached, on the river front; and a range of lesser bedrooms on the road front. Throughout the house were handsome cornices, plaster flowers in the ceilings and fine marble fireplaces. The basement contained the usual array of kitchens, servants' hall, butler's and housekeeper's rooms and a dairy.

By the time Douglas and his family moved into the house in 1828, quantities of furniture had been

After John Woolford: Road Front Elevation of Government House, Fredericton. Copy by J.H. Brigly, 1907, of the drawing in the Public Record Office, London.

After John Woolford: River Front Elevation of Government House, Fredericton. Copy by J.H. Brigly, 1907, of the drawing in the Public Record Office, London.

travels of 1821 in British North America. While in Halifax with his patron, he had made lithographic views of the Government House there. And so, when Government House, Fredericton, caught fire in September 1825, and all but the rear wing and the furniture was destroyed, a designer was on hand to plan a replacement. Douglas meanwhile lived in a rented house.

Nor was the Assembly loath to vote funds in 1826 for the new house,[58] the grandeur of which was the province's greatest tribute to the Governor's popularity. The cornerstone was laid on 1 July, the plans were ready the following year, and the house was finished by December 1828.

Woolford's designs show his dependence on the Hildrith-Adam-Richardson ones for Halifax. The walls on both fronts of the house are solid masses of cut stone, into which large windows are punched at regular intervals, with smaller ones to light the servants' rooms

Government House, Fredericton: the Portico. Photograph 1984.

John Woolford(?): Government House, Fredericton, from the St John River. Etching, c.1825.

bought to supplement what had been rescued from the fire. Most of the new pieces came from Nisbet[59] though some were ordered from London, presumably from the Seddon firm of cabinetmakers. The partial list which follows is derived from an inventory made prior to the sale of 1897[60] and appears to include the original furniture:

> *In the drawing room:* mahogany chairs, easy chairs, walnut lounges, card tables, a chandelier, an overmantel looking-glass and a light drab Brussels carpet.
> *In the dining room:* a large sectional banquet table,[61] two dozen walnut chairs, four small square tables, two mahogany sideboards, a rosewood sideboard, rosewood lounges and mahogany sofas.

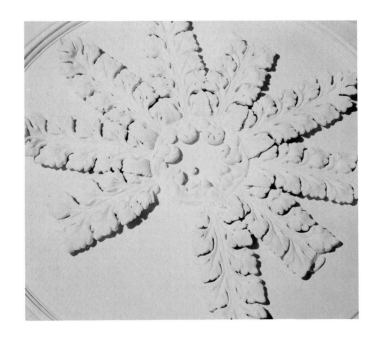

In the ballroom: a mahogany table, mahogany and walnut chairs, overmantel looking-glasses and a Brussels carpet.

In the library: a mahogany davenport and easy chairs, two card tables, a whatnot, a walnut davenport and bookcases.

In the council room: a mahogany table and lounge and chintz-covered chairs.

In the governor's room: a square mahogany table, an armchair, four mahogany chairs, a butternut square table, a small walnut table, bookcases and three brass chandeliers.

In the hall: tables, lounges, a dozen mahogany chairs and a stove.

The lesser rooms above and below stairs contained simpler furniture as well as such cast-offs as (in 1895) a "lounge demoralized" in the pantry.[61]

Government House became the cynosure of all eyes in the province. Douglas's successor Sir John Harvey only outdid him, holding dinners three evenings a week and a ball every fortnight. Everything was done in state. His Sunday morning churchgoing was accomplished in the State carriage accompanied by a band. But he also held popular entertainments, most notably for the Indians on New Year's Day. One who had known the Indian leader Joe Sebatis, describes a dance performed by the "warriors" in full costume with embroidered belts, each carrying a knife. They faced inwards in a circle round their chief, and their movements became quicker until Sebatis feared a demonic outburst.[62]

In the grounds behind the house were clumps of tall trees framing a formal garden, which was separated by fences from the terrace and the river bank. It was here, in 1832, in Sir Archibald Campbell's time, that the visiting Audubon sketched the pine finch (pine siskin) which appeared as a plate in *Birds of America** (1835-8).

In the prosperous years at the middle of the nineteenth century the successive governors of New Brunswick maintained their house in state and comfort. From it, in 1845, the unpopular Sir William Colebrook went to lay the cornerstone of Bishop Medley's new cathedral designed by Frank Wills; it was the first great monument of Tractarianism and of the Gothic Revival in Canada. Sir Edmund Head, the wise and cultivated governor of the years from 1848 to 1854, was an amateur artist who made plans and sepia views of the house and grounds.[63]

As in other capitals, the great event of the century was the Prince of Wales's visit in 1860.[64] In preparation

**Plate 180 in the elephant folio.*

Government House, Fredericton: Plaster Ceiling Ornament. Photograph 1984.

83

John Woolford: Government House, Fredericton. Etching.

for this event many items of furniture "of the latest style" were bought in Saint John, Liverpool and Boston. Chief among them was a great bed (now in the York-Sunbury Historical Society) with a crimson damask canopy and the Prince's feathers crowning its posts. There were also gilt window cornices, new table silver and the gilding of the finials on the two summer-houses in the grounds. The young Prince during his stay inaugurated a new park in Fredericton with a fountain which, it is said, refused to function for the

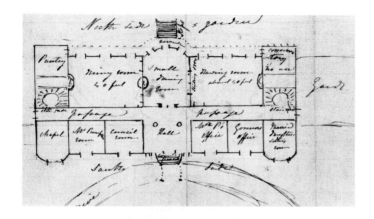

occasion. At another time he escaped from the house to join an Indian canoe party on the river and visited a Malecite chief. After his departure a canny Assembly auctioned off the extra furnishings they had bought for the occasion. All this happened in the period of Sir John Manners-Sutton, who was popular in his day for the variety of his entertainments.

The next governor was Arthur Hamilton Gordon who received not only his own nephew Lord Haddo (later 6th Earl of Aberdeen and brother of the future governor general of Canada) but Prince Alfred, Duke of Edinburgh, Queen Victoria's second son. But

Sir Edmund Head, Bt: Sketch Plan of the Ground Floor of Government House, Fredericton. Pen Drawing, c.1848-54.

Sir Edmund Head, Bt: The River Front of Government House, Fredericton. Pen Drawing, c.1848-54.

Sleigh in front of Government House, Fredericton. Photograph 1870s.

Gordon's chief importance lies in the part he played in the Confederation debate. Instructed by London to press for it for reasons of defence, he faced the opposition of an anti-Confederation government, and in 1866 held the stormy interview with its leader Albert J. Smith, which precipitated the fall of the administration and opened up the way to union.

After Confederation the lieutenant governors of the provinces were appointed by the federal government. For the ensuing thirty-five years these men kept up the house to the degree of state which had been established by the governors from Britain. The number of important visitors increased with the improvement of transportation. Though Prince Arthur in 1869 arrived in Fredericton by steamboat, Sir John A. Macdonald in 1873 came by rail, in Sir Leonard Tilley's

Government House, Fredericton, with Greenhouse. Photograph by George Taylor, c.1890.

Sir Leonard Tilley's Sons in the Greenhouse, Government House, Fredericton. Stereoscopic photograph, c.1885.

first governorship, to attend the opening of the Canada Eastern Railway's link with Montreal. Lord and Lady Dufferin reverted to river steamer when they made their official visit in 1873. After their greeting at the landing stage by Lemuel Allan Wilmot, Lady Dufferin found Government House "a very good one; the river passes the house, and a very pretty flower garden goes down to it".[65] In 1879, in Edward Barron Chandler's time, Lord Lorne and Princess Louise came to stay, later to be followed by the Lansdownes and Stanleys.

Government House was the first in a melancholy series of closings of official residences in the provinces. For New Brunswick, the latter part of the nineteenth century, after the passing of the era of "wood, wind and sail", was a period of particular hardship and of disillusionment with Confederation. Economy in expenditure by the provincial government was the motive invoked for the closing of the house in 1893, during

Tilley's second period in office. A stereoscopic photograph of his sons taken in the greenhouse (which had been added beside the house) is a last sad document of the life that had been led in the place for more than sixty years. Lady Aberdeen, on her visit to Fredericton with her husband in August 1894, wrote in her diary, "It seems a great pity to let it decay, as it appears a charming English kind of house, with well proportioned rooms & very comfortable".[66]

An inventory of the contents of the house having been prepared in 1895, an auction was held in 1897. Mixed in with the original furnishings were numerous Victorian items which had been acquired in the meantime. These included cases of stuffed birds, gasoliers with glass globes, rocking chairs, patent stoves, a water closet, marble-topped tables, a refrigerator and a "pair of fine vases with Governors' portraits". The sale fetched the shockingly low total of $2000.[67]

Government House, Fredericton: the Road Front. Photograph by Shackleton, 1960s.

The pieces were bought by some of the leading families, and it has been possible to trace a number of them.[68]

After the closing the lieutenant governors of New Brunswick were obliged to live in hotels or rented houses. Jabez Snowball, in the period from 1902 to 1907, leased the only house in Fredericton with a ball-room. Such arrangements were detrimental to the incumbent's position and his ability to carry out his hospitable and social duties. Prince Jérôme Bonaparte, the grand-nephew of the Emperor, stayed in Tilley's own house which, in his own frank words, was "a very nice house indeed, but oh! not suitable for the governor of a large Province like this".[69] Lord and

had been removed and extensive temporary wings added, which disfigured its lines. In another period of vacancy, from 1924 to 1934, the temporary wings were removed, and in the latter year it became the regional headquarters of the Royal Canadian Mounted Police. At some point the small windows in the attic storey were enlarged into dormers which broke the roof line and spoiled the unity of the total design of the house.

With the return of comparative prosperity to the province in recent years efforts have been made to house the lieutenant governor in more appropriate style. Somerville House[71] in Waterloo Row was first occupied by the Hon. Hédard Robichaud in 1974 and thus became the third Government House in Fredericton. This house, originally built in the 1820s by John Murray Bliss, is on the evidence of its architectural details a possible design by John Woolford and may thus form a link with the great house. But it has suffered many changes over the years. Its roof was altered after a fire in 1867; and with its various appendages it came to resemble a "Queen Anne" house of the late nineteenth century. At some time after 1905 it was bequeathed to the University of New Brunswick, which resold it in 1909. In 1948 Lord Beaverbrook, Fredericton's great benefactor, bought it and gave it back to the University, which used it as a law school until 1968. When the province decided to make it into an official residence it was furnished in period pieces, including some from old Government House.

Meanwhile the great house had not been forgotten. A garden party was held in its grounds for the Queen and Prince Philip in 1959. More recently an extensive collection of furniture has been in formation pending its eventual restoration. Certain pieces of the original furniture have been recovered from private collections and others have been identified in the Legislative Building.

Government House (Somerville House), Fredericton. Photograph c.1977.

Lady Minto stayed in a hotel, and the Duke and Duchess of Cornwall and York in 1901 could not even visit the capital for lack of accommodation.

Since 1893 old Government House has had a chequered career, in spite of which it still stands intact. From 1896 to 1900 it served as a provincial school for the deaf and dumb. After an interval of vacancy, during which there was a vain attempt on the part of Lady Aberdeen's Local Council of Women to restore it to its proper use,[70] it became a military hospital during the First World War, after which time it was bought by the federal government and used as a veterans' hospital until 1924. By this time the veranda and the greenhouse

Dr George Stanley and Mrs Stanley in Government House, Fredericton, Photograph 1984.

Their Honours Gilbert Finn and Mrs Finn in Government House, Fredericton.

Government House (Somerville House), Fredericton: the Dining Room, with table by Thomas Nisbet from Old Government House. Photograph 1983.

A complete restoration is now contemplated, but this cannot be embarked upon until the federal authority provides new quarters for the RCMP. Old Government House appears to be in remarkably good condition — a tribute to the solidity of its construction and the care taken by its tenants. Though the larger rooms have been partitioned into offices, they retain enough of their cornices, fireplaces and other details to make restoration relatively easy. The main problem is that the house is too large for the exclusive use of a lieutenant governor today, lacking an adequate staff to run it. A possible solution to the problem, suggested by the examples of two western provinces, is for the provincial government to share in the use of the State rooms for official functions, and for the lieutenant governor to have his private apartment in one wing.

It is greatly hoped that some such plan may be adopted, which will allow one of the country's great houses to be once more in operation and preserved for posterity. Under Dr George Stanley and, I am sure, under the present incumbent His Honour Gilbert Finn, both deeply interested in their province's heritage, solutions have been sought which will both enhance the dignity of the Crown and express the bicultural nature of New Brunswick.

Lieutenant Governors of New Brunswick 1784-1867

Thomas Carleton (1735-1817)	1784-1817
George Stracey Smyth (1767?-1823)	1817-1823
Sir Howard Douglas, Bt (1776-1861)	1824-1831
Sir Archibald Campbell, Bt (1769-1843)	1831-1837
Sir John Harvey (1778-1852)	1837-1841
Sir William MacBean George Colebrook (1787-1870)	1841-1848
Sir Edmund Walker Head, Bt (1805-1868)	1848-1854
Sir John Manners-Sutton, Viscount Canterbury (1814-1877)	1854-1861
Arthur Hamilton Gordon, later Lord Stanmore (1819-1912)	1861-1866
Sir Charles Hastings Doyle (1804-1883)	1866-1867

Lieutenant Governors of the Province of New Brunswick 1867-

Francis Pym Harding (c.1821-1875)	1867-1868
Lemuel Allan Wilmot (1809-1878)	1868-1873
Sir Samuel Leonard Tilley (1818-1896)	1873-1878 and 1885-1893
Edward Barron Chandler (1800-1880)	1878-1880
Robert Duncan Wilmot (1809-1891)	1880-1885
John Boyd (1826-1893)	1893
John James Fraser (1829-1896)	1893-1896
Abner Reid McClelan (1831-1917)	1896-1902
Jabez Bunting Snowball (1837-1907)	1902-1907
Lemuel John Tweedie (1849-1917)	1907-1912
Josiah Wood (1843-1927)	1912-1917
Gilbert White Ganong (1851-1917)	1917
William Pugsley (1850-1925)	1917-1923
William Freeman Todd (1854-1935)	1923-1928
Hugh Havelock McLean (1854-1938)	1928-1935
Murray MacLaren (1861-1942)	1935-1940
William George Clark (1865-1948)	1940-1945
David Lawrence MacLaren (1893-1960)	1945-1958
Joseph Leonard O'Brien (1895-	1958-1965
John Babbitt McNair (1889-	1965-1968
Wallace Samuel Bird (1917-1971)	1968-1971
Hédard-Joseph Robichaud (1911-	1971-1981
George F.G. Stanley (1907–	1982-1987
Gilbert Finn (1920–	1987

*G*overnment House, Charlottetown.
Photograph 1860s.

Prince Edward Island

Prince Edward Island made its first appearance in history as Île Saint-Jean, a fisheries concession to the French colonial enterprisers. Later it served as an agricultural outpost of Île Royale, supplying food to the fortress of Louisbourg on the rocky Cape Breton shore. But only a few of the French settlers had survived famine and plague by the time the island first fell to the British in 1745. Restored to France in 1748, it fell a second time, along with Louisbourg, in 1758. By the Treaty of Paris in 1763 it was ceded to the British and annexed to Nova Scotia. By 1765, on Hillsborough Bay, the site for a capital, to be named Charlottetown after the consort of George III, had been chosen.

As a British possession, St John's Island differed from the rest of the northern provinces not only by its small size but (as in some of the Thirteen Colonies) by its division into tracts granted to absentee proprietors in England. Few of the landlords ever developed their land, and the land question was to plague the island for many years to come.

In 1769 the colony was detached from Nova Scotia to form a separate province and was provided with the full panoply of colonial government — and all for a population of some two hundred and fifty souls. The first governor, Colonel Walter Patterson,* arrived the following summer. While he was in office settlers began to arrive, notably the Loyalists in the 1780s; and with them began the development of agriculture and commerce. In 1799 the province's name was changed to Prince Edward Island in honour of Edward, Duke of Kent, who had just been made commander-in-chief of the forces in British North America. Patterson had

Governor from 1769 to 1784 and lieutenant governor from 1784 to 1787.

meanwhile, in 1787, left the island in disgrace following a scandal over an affair with the wife of the chief justice of the day.

It was his successor, Edmund Fanning, the Loyalist lieutenant governor from 1787 to 1804, who chose the pretty site for his official residence, in a hundred acres of birch wood on the harbour at a little distance from town. But he and three of his successors lived in temporary quarters until the arrival in 1831 of Sir Aretas Young, a veteran officer of the Peninsular War. The year after his arrival, after an assessment on land had been authorized by the Colonial Office to provide the funds, Young appointed a commission to supervise the building of his house.[72]

Tenders were called in September 1832 "for building a Government House at Fanning Bank", and the contract was awarded to three Charlottetown builders, Isaac and Henry Smith and Nathan Wright, at a cost of £2858.11s., with the proviso that the building should be finished by 1 December 1834.[73]

The author of the plans is unknown, but it may be assumed he was one of the builders who was not only carrying out the lieutenant governor's ideas but relying on his own familiarity with the modes and manners of timber building in other parts of the Atlantic coast. More specifically, the design of the house shows a general influence of the English Regency style; and Isaac Smith was later to prepare the Regency Italianate plans for Province House in Charlottetown.

Thus Government House had the ample, rectangular shape of its period. Its white walls were shingled in the traditional New England and Maritimes manner. The door on the harbour front of the house had a small porch with a fanlight and was flanked by pilasters. A gallery ran round three sides, its entablature supported on wooden Doric columns. But the salient feature was a monumental Ionic portico with a pediment, rising over the central portion of the façade

Anonymous: Sir Aretas Young.

A.E. Santagnello: Government House, Prince Edward Island. Drawing, c.1852.

to the full height of the house. A smaller entrance on the east side gave access to the governor's waiting room, and wings at the back housed the domestic offices. Viewed from the harbour or from the east across the little bridge spanning the outlet of Government Pond the mansion stood out from its sylvan setting like a temple in Arcadia, as did other houses of the period in England and America.

The interior plan was simplicity itself. The principal rooms on both floors were grouped round a spacious central court which extended to the top of the house and afforded a large space on the ground floor for State functions. A broad stair facing the door divided into two at a landing which, with its Palladian window, provided an effective ceremonial focus for the hall. Fluted Ionic columns supported a gallery and this colonnade was repeated on the upper floor on a smaller scale. The Neo-Classic cornices in this and the other state rooms were the subject of a spirited competition between two plasterers, Chudleigh and Connell, as to which was the better craftsman.[74]

The rooms on the ground floor were, to left of the door, the drawing room and dining room, and to right the governor's study (now a private drawing room), the secretary's office (now the lieutenant governor's study), the pantry and servants' hall (now a private dining room). Upstairs, all principal bedrooms opened into the gallery. Those on the south front (the Queen's Room on the left and the lieutenant governor's on the right) overlooked the harbour.

The furniture was ordered (as in New Brunswick) from Thomas and George Seddon, the fashionable London cabinetmakers of the day. As reported to the House of Assembly in 1835, the furnishings included the following items:

In the hall: six "fly" chairs with cane seats, a large ormolu hanging lamp, chintz curtains in "shawl" pattern, lined with green, a Brussels carpet and patent oil floor cloth, thirty yards of stair carpet, wallpaper and a "large handsome stove".

In the drawing room: two mahogany card tables "on massive pillars and triangular plinths, ball feet and castors", a loo table, a mahogany occasional table, a sofa table, two large curved sofas, a dozen Trafalgar chairs with red-striped seats, two pier-glasses (now in the hall), an ormolu spout lamp, red-stripe chintz curtains with fringe, a Brussels carpet and bordered wallpaper.

In the dining room: a mahogany telescope table for twenty-four with "massive turned and channelled legs", eighteen mahogany scroll-top chairs covered in morocco, a large mahogany sideboard "with pedestal ends, a pediment shape back board on top, with carved pattern ornament", a chimney glass, scarlet moreen curtains with fringe, a Brussels carpet, figured wallpaper and an antique spout lamp.[75]

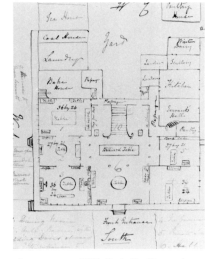

Anonymous (J.W. Daly?): Ground Floor Plan of Government House, Charlottetown. Ink drawing, c.1856.

Government House, Charlottetown: the Dining Room. Photograph 1983.

Government House, Charlottetown: the Small Drawing Room. Photograph 1983.

Also in the house at present are two pieces of furniture by the Charlottetown cabinetmaker Mark Butcher: a reading chair and a washstand with marble top and carved back rail.

The first important event to take place in the new house was a ball held in January 1837 by the lieutenant governor of the day, Sir John Harvey* — for Young had died in 1835 shortly after moving in. As reported in the *Royal Gazette,*

Afterwards governor of Bermuda, Newfoundland and Nova Scotia

An entertainment, upon a grand and splendid scale, was given by His Excellency, Sir John and Lady Harvey at Government House on Thursday evening last; and as this was the first occasion upon which the rooms at Government House were thrown open to a large evening party, no pains were spared to give full effect to the enlivening scene. His Excellency and Lady Harvey received their guests in the centre drawing room, and at ten o'clock dancing commenced, which was continued with great spirit and animation until after one o'clock. The rooms were brilliantly lighted, and this, added to the crown of beauty and fashion with which they were thronged, exhibited their handsome proportions to peculiar advantage.[76]

A wedding reception in August 1841 was an equally splendid affair. It took place in the time of Sir Charles FitzRoy, a grandson of the Duke of Grafton, and lieutenant governor from 1837 to 1841. The bride was his daughter Mary Caroline, and the bridegroom the Hon. (later Admiral) Keith Stewart, a son of the Earl of Galloway. Seventy or eighty guests partook of a *déjeuner à la fourchette* in the central hall, and the healths of the couple were drunk in bumpers of champagne.

The following year certain repairs and alterations were made to the house. Partitions were erected to make a dining room out of the front part of the drawing room, and a wine cellar and "closet" were formed in the old dining room. By this time a post-and-rail fence enclosed the park,[77] and flower gardens had been laid out to the west of the house, set off to advantage against the birch wood.

But the lieutenant governor of that day, Henry Vere Huntley, was at odds with the oligarchy. When the Executive Council turned down his request for a guard of soldiers at the approaches to the house, he retaliated by withdrawing his patronage from various institutions in the province.

It was a different story in 1851, when Sir Alexander Bannerman, the jovial Whig who had married a Charlottetown wife, rejoiced in the province's achievement of responsible government. He greeted a torchlight procession of the victorious Reform party by lighting up every window of Government House. But he too fell foul of his Council and was recalled to England in 1854, only to endure greater turbulence as governor of Newfoundland several years later.

As in other provinces, the great event of the period was the visit of the Prince of Wales in 1860. A splendid welcome arch with representations of soldiers and dancing girls was put up opposite Government

J.W. Daly: The Central Hall (Billiard Room), Government House, Charlottetown. Water colour.

Government House, Charlottetown: the Central Hall.

Government House, Charlottetown: The Queen's Bedroom. Photograph 1983.

John Coory Wilson Daly: Government House — Winter Scene. *Water colour, 1856.*

House.[78] George Dundas as occupant of the house provided a guard of honour and fêted the Prince in a round of dinners and balls during his short stay. Charlottetown attracted the passing attention of the English public when an engraved view of Government House, after a drawing by G.H. Andrews, appeared in *Illustrated London News.*[79]

For the history of Canada, however, the major event of the period was the Charlottetown Conference of 1864, at which uninvited delegates from the province of Canada diverted the purpose of the gathering from Maritime union to the confederation of all the provinces of British North America. Their deliberations led to the Quebec Conference of the same year; and the movement was under way. Dundas entertained the delegates at an opening dinner and later at a ball which George Brown of the Toronto *Globe* described as "a very nice affair, but a great bore for old fellows like me".[80] All the delegates, wearing or holding their stove-pipe hats, posed under the portico of Government House for the famous photograph in which, significantly, John A. Macdonald and George-Étienne Cartier occupied the centre of the group.

Prince Edward Island's entry into Confederation in 1873 was tardy and reluctant. For the inauguration of the new province, Lord and Lady Dufferin arrived by ship in July and were welcomed by the lieutenant governor of the day, Sir William Robinson. Characteristically, Lady Dufferin recorded the more picturesque aspects of the visit in her journal: an arch in town bearing the inscription "Long courted, won at last", a drive through "red lanes, farms, trees and ferns, country sites which are quite delightful to us, who of late have only seen forest scenery", a regatta in the

THE VISIT OF THE PRINCE OF WALES TO NORTH AMERICA.—THE GOVERNMENT HOUSE, CHARLOTTE TOWN, PRINCE EDWARD ISLAND.

After G.N. Andrews: The Visit of the Prince of Wales to . . . Government House, Charlotte Town. *Wood-engraving in* Illustrated London News, *4 August 1860.*

harbour and a trip on the new island railway. At the ball in Government House one pretty girl accused the Governor General's A.D.C. of having danced only with the plain girls. And on the night of their departure, after a ball in the Confederation Chamber, there was a torchlight procession to the ship, with the ladies in their ball dresses waving farewell from the balcony of Province House.[81]

At this time Government House was still outside the town. An agricultural exhibition hall had recently been built just across Government Pond, and for a good many years the judging of livestock took place in the rural setting of the lieutenant governor's grounds.

The official visits of governors general of Canada became regular events with the improvement of communications in the latter part of the century. The

The Delegates to the Charlottetown Conference, in front of Government House, Charlottetown. Photograph by G.P. Roberts, 1864.

Government House, Charlottetown.
Photograph 1890s.

Dance Programme, Government House, Charlottetown (a and b), 1894.

grandest visitors of all were the Marquess of Lorne and Princess Louise in 1879. Though they stayed aboard their ship, and though a great storm sent swirling eddies of red dust into the air, the Princess, always discriminating, remarked that had she known how nice and comfortable Government House was, they would have stayed there.[82] Yet it was at about this time, to judge from old photographs, that the house sacrificed some of its arcadian charm, when the original round columns of the portico were replaced by square ones, little more than posts.

In spite of the appointment of lieutenant governors by the ruling party in Ottawa, life at Government House continued through the late nineteenth century and well into the twentieth in the traditional way. A ball programme dating from the régime of George Howlan (1894-1899) includes old-fashioned waltzes, lancers, polkas and galops to music by favourite Victorian composers, the only recognizable name among them being that of Émile Waldteufel. On Lady Aberdeen's visit in August 1894 she had nothing but praise for Government House: "a nice old fashioned house commanding fine view of harbour & our hosts [the Howlans] are most kind & considerate". But on a later visit, in October 1897, she noted that Howlan was "a regular old character & is not very popular because he does not entertain much". At a dinner party he "tried our gravity by suddenly proposing the Queen's health between the first & second courses".[83]

After visits from the effusive Lord Grey ("every province in turn captured his heart"[84]) in 1910, and later from the Duke of Connaught and his beautiful and talented daughter Princess Patricia, a period of sobriety was ushered in by the First World War. By the time of the Duke of Devonshire's first visit in December 1918, the lieutenant governor, Augustine Colin Macdonald, had handed over his house to the military authorities for use as a convalescent hospital.

A temporary building added to the east end of the house accommodated two hundred beds. "Must have been a charming house," wrote the Duke in his diary, "well situated on the river". On his next visit, in July 1920, the grounds were the setting for a garden party in his honour.[85] In this wartime and postwar interval such capable lieutenant governors as Frank Richard Heartz maintained as high a degree of state as was possible in their own houses, tempered by the Island flavour that is suggested by the salmon, native turkey, lobster salad and strawberry shortcake in one of the dinner menus of the 1920s.[86]

Visit of Lord and Lady Grey to Charlottetown, 1910: the Lieutenant Governor in carriage at centre.

By 1932 the temporary wing had been removed and the house had reverted to its proper function. In spite of the depression George Des Brisay De Blois, who succeeded to office the following year, was able to send out Christmas cards showing the central hall charmingly decorated for the holiday season. The numerous visits in the 1930s from officers of Royal Navy ships anchored in Charlottetown harbour provided cheerful occasions on which to entertain members of such Island families as the Popes, Hyndmans, Le Pages, Carvells, Rogerses and Warburtons.

It was in 1937, also in the De Blois period, that Lord Tweedsmuir paid his viceregal visit to "this delectable island".[87] His private observations are on record:

It is the old Canada of half a century ago. There is no great wealth and no great poverty, and there is no distinction between town and country. The whole place is really a village community. A pleasanter or a quainter society could hardly be imagined. The atmosphere is like that of Cranford. At the party which the

The Duke of Connaught and Princess Patricia at Charlottetown, 1912.

Lieutenant-Governor gave for me local talent performed with recitations and songs — songs and recitations which were new about 1850. It is a secure and happy little community desperately British in spirit, and I felt during my visit as if I had suddenly been transplanted to a Scottish parish.[88]

A less attractive side of provincialism is reflected in the action of one lieutenant governor, Bradford W. Le Page, who withheld assent to a bill liberalizing the province's liquor laws. This he did because of his personal teetotalism; and the constitutional stir that arose was not ended until his successor Joseph Bernard assented to a new bill.

Meanwhile the most important visit before the Second World War had taken place when King George VI and Queen Elizabeth arrived in the Island in 1939. On that occasion, however, the garden party was rained upon, and Government House gave shelter to as many guests as could crowd in. Since the war the Queen and Prince Philip have come a number of times, most notably in 1964 for the opening of the Fathers of Confederation Building in Charlottetown. The present writer well remembers this and the other celebrations of the centenary of the Charlottetown Conference for their unique blend of splendour and informality in the best Island tradition. To the growing number of royal and viceregal visits have been added those of numerous ambassadors of foreign countries.

In recent years Government House has been restored and furnished with the help of a committee representing both good taste and historical knowledge. Thus the Queen's Room on the harbour front now contains a fine four-poster bed and other period furniture. Under the aegis of Dr Aubin Doiron, the second lieutenant governor of Acadian descent, and of the present occupant the Hon. Robert McPhail, the old house carries its old traditions into the latter part of the twentieth century, adapting them to new conditions and providing a focus for Island pride and aspirations.

His Honour Robert McPhail, Lieutenant Governor of Prince Edward Island.

Lieutenant Governors of Prince Edward Island 1769-1873

Walter Patterson (c.1735-1798)	1769-1787
Edmund Fanning (1737-1818)	1787-1804
Joseph Frederic Wallet Des Barres (1722-1824)	1805-1812
Charles Douglas Smith (fl.1812-1824)	1812-1824
John Ready (d.1845)	1824-1831
Sir Aretas William Young (c.1778-1835)	1831-1835
Sir John Harvey (1778-1852)	1836-1837
Sir Charles Augustus FitzRoy (1796-1858)	1837-1841
Sir Henry Vere Huntley (1795-1864)	1841-1847
Sir Donald Campbell, Bt (1800-1850)	1847-1850
Sir Alexander Bannerman (1788-1864)	1850-1854
Sir Dominick Daly (1798-1868)	1854-1859
George Dundas (1819-1880)	1859-1868
William Robinson (1834-1897)	1870-1873

Lieutenant Governors of the Province of Prince Edward Island 1873-

Sir Robert Hodgson (1798-1880)	1873-1879
Thomas Heath Haviland (1822-1895)	1879-1884
Andrew Archibald Macdonald (1829-1912)	1884-1889
Jedediah Slason Carvell (1832-1894)	1889-1894
George William Howlan (1835-1901)	1894-1899
Peter Adolphus McIntyre (1840-1910)	1899-1904
Donald Alexander MacKinnon (1863-1928)	1904-1910
Benjamin Rogers (1837-1927)	1910-1915
Augustine Colin Macdonald (1837-1919)	1915-1919
Murdoch McKinnon (1865-1944)	1919-1924
Frank Richard Heartz (1871-1955)	1924-1930
Sir Charles Dalton (1850-1933)	1930-1933
George Des Brisay De Blois (1887-1964)	1933-1939
Bradford William Le Page (1867-1958)	1939-1945
Joseph Alphonsus Bernard (1881-1962)	1945-1950
Thomas William Lemuel Prowse (1888-	1950-1958
Frederick Walter Hyndman (1904-	1958-1963
Willibald Joseph MacDonald (1897-	1963-1969
John George McKay	1969-1974
Gordon Lockhart Bennett (1912-	1974-1980
Joseph-Aubin Doiron (1923-	1980-1985
Robert Lloyd George McPhail (1920-	1985

P A R T F O U R

Upper Canada & Ontario

The Early Years: Niagara and Toronto
A Victorian Mansion
Chorley Park

*G*overnment House, Toronto: the
Lieutenant Governor's Bedroom.
From a half-tone, c.1903-8.

The Early Years: Niagara and Toronto

The province of Upper Canada was formed under the provisions of the Constitutional Act of 1791, by which the old province of Quebec was divided into Upper and Lower Canada, with the Ottawa River as their boundary. In the seventeen years following the Quebec Act of 1774 the Loyalists arriving from the western parts of the American colonies, and including the Indians of the Six Nations, had changed a fur-trading hinterland of the St Lawrence colony into an English-speaking settlement. The Act of 1791 satisfied the desire of the new population for its own elected Assembly.

The first lieutenant governor of Upper Canada, under the governor at Quebec, was Colonel John Graves Simcoe, who had commanded the Queen's Rangers in the war of the American Revolution until taken prisoner in Virginia. In the new province he quickly established the framework of government and in 1792, the year of his arrival, convoked the first Assembly at Newark (Niagara-on-the-Lake), the point at which many of the Loyalists were crossing into Canada. There Simcoe and his wife lived in Navy Hall, a cluster of frame buildings which had been used for stores and as winter quarters for the lake sailors.

In 1793 Simcoe transferred his capital to Toronto, the site of an Indian village and an old French fort, and gave it the name of York in honour of the Duke of York and Albany, the second son of George III. The following year he began construction of a government building, the middle wing of which was to have been his official residence.[1] But as the wing was never built, he took shelter in the famous "canvas houses" he had bought from the estate of Captain James Cook. In 1795 he built for himself a one-storeyed summer retreat on the wooded banks of the Don River. This house is the subject of several of Mrs Simcoe's drawings and of an entry in her diary for 1796:

Elizabeth Simcoe: Castle-Frank near York. *Pen and wash on birchbark, c.1795.*

It is called Castle Frank built on the plan of a Grecian temple, totally of wood the Logs squared & so grooved together that in case of decay any log may be taken out. The large Pine trees make Pillars for the Porticos which are at each end 16 feet high.[2]

The first house with a claim to the name of Government House was built in 1800 in Fort York for Simcoe's successor Peter Hunter, a brother of the great London surgeon and anatomist John Hunter. As lieutenant governor from 1799 to 1805 Hunter was also commander of the forces in the two Canadas and spent much of his time away from York. As a result the government was left largely to his Council. His house was a very plain one-storeyed frame affair designed for him by Lieutenant Robert Pilkington (1765-1834) of the Royal Engineers. It had three rooms on the front and other rooms in two wings at the back.[3] As George Heriot, deputy postmaster-general of British North America and an artist, remarked, the house was "sufficiently commodious for the present state of the province, and is erected upon a bank of the lake, near the mouth of Toronto Bay".[3a]

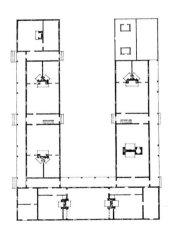

Plan and elevation of the Lieutenant Governor's House, York, built by Captain Robert Pilkington, 1800.

Simcoe's policy of encouraging the land-hungry of the United States to settle in Upper Canada resulted in an influx of "Yankees", whose numbers nearly equalled those of the original settlers. The outcome of all this was a strong leaning towards a democratic form of government, which in turn led to the political strife of a later day. But the character of Upper Canada was also moulded by the actions of the War of 1812 which took place on its own soil and gave rise to a tradition of local patriotism and strong loyalty to the Crown.

The war had a drastic effect on the first Government House of Upper Canada, which by this time was occupied by the high-handed Francis Gore. It was destroyed in the explosion of the powder magazine in Fort York during the American raid of April 1813 — "the moment they got in".[3b] In retaliation for this deed the British later burned the White House in Washington.

Charles John Colville, 1st Viscount Colville of Culross: Government House (Elmsley), Toronto. *Wash drawing, 1840.*

It was only after the war had ended that the province gave thought to a replacement. Through its London agent the Assembly approached the great architect of the English Regency, Sir John Soane. The sketch plan he drew in 1818[4] shows his characteristic circular vestibule and staircases. Typical too of his style was an elevation with a pedimented central block of two storeys flanked by identical one-storeyed wings. Though this design was never executed in York, it seems in some curious way to have influenced Rideau Hall (1838) in backwoods Bytown, the unique example in Canada of a Soane villa.[5]

The problem of a residence at York was solved instead by the purchase of Elmsley,[6] a house which the Chief Justice of Upper Canada John Elmsley had built in 1798 on a tract of land bounded by the present King, Simcoe, Wellington and John streets. Having served as a hospital during the War of 1812, the house had escaped destruction. Later it constituted one of the famous Four Corners at King and Simcoe streets, representing Government along with Upper Canada College (Education), St. Andrew's Church (Salvation) and the British Tavern (Damnation). Elmsley House, which Gore was the first to occupy, was a Regency Italianate villa with spreading eaves and tall corniced windows.

Charles John Colville, 1st Viscount Colville of Culross: Bottom of the Gardens, Govt. House (Elmsley), Toronto. *Detail of a wash drawing, c.1840.*

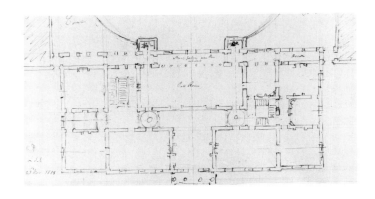

Sir John Soane: Sketch Plan for a Government House at York, Upper Canada. Drawing, 1818.

Under Gore's successor Sir Peregrine Maitland, the son-in-law of the Duke of Richmond, a greenhouse and a ballroom were added to the house in 1819. A ball held in the latter room eighteen years later, in Sir Francis Bond Head's régime, is described by Anna Jameson, the English art historian who was the wife of the vice-chancellor of Upper Canada:

> Last night a ball at the Government House, to which people came from a distance of fifty — a hundred — two hundred miles — which is nothing to signify here. There were very pretty girls, and very nice dancing; but

Hoppner Meyer: Lord Sydenham.
Detail of an engraving, 1842.

we had all too much reason to lament the loss of the band of the 66th regiment, which left us a few weeks ago — to my sorrow.

It is to be hoped that all the governors sent here for the future may be married men, and bring their wives with them, for the presence of a female at the head of our little provincial court — particularly if she be intelligent, good-natured, and accomplished — is a greater advantage to the society here, and does more to render the government popular, than you can well imagine.[7]

In 1838 a new ballroom was designed for Sir George Arthur by the Toronto architect John George Howard (1803-1890). Also during Arthur's period (1834-1841) his aide-de-camp Captain John (later Lord) Colville made two pencil-and-wash views of Elmsley and its picturesque wooded grounds with a winding brook.[8]

Government House, Toronto — the city had reverted to its original name in 1834 — suffered from the vagaries of the Canadian politics of the period. The Rebellion of 1837 against the colonial oligarchy was followed by Lord Durham's recommendation of responsible government and the union of the two Canadas. When these were accomplished in 1841, the house ceased to have a reason for being, for the capital of Canada now began its sojourns in one town and another in order to appease local jealousies.

In 1841 Kingston was chosen, and three governors general, Lord Sydenham, Sir Charles Bagot and Lord Metcalfe, resided at Alwington, a stone villa which had been built in 1839 by Charles William Grant, son of the Baroness de Longueuil. Both Sydenham and Bagot died in Kingston. The house was a handsome example

of Regency Italianate, with its central block treated as an Ionic temple portico. Frame additions designed by the Montreal architect George Browne (fl. 1831-54) provided the necessary state apartments and offices. Charles Dickens, who visited Kingston in 1842, considered it "a very poor town" and (mistakenly) Alwington as "neither elegant nor commodious".[9] Perversely he chose to admire a prison as the town's best building. Alwington survived until fire destroyed it in 1958. In its heyday it contained some pretty

furniture including a rosewood table and a sofa covered in cherry and white.

After a four-year stay in Kingston the government removed to Montreal where it remained until after the riots of 1849. When it returned to Toronto in that year, Elmsley House was not available, having been made into a normal school with a part of its grounds sold off. And so the governor general of the day, Lord Elgin, was installed in Elmsley Villa,[10] a house which had been built in 1839 for a son-in-law of the Chief Justice. Another Italianate villa, it was set in broad grounds in the northern outskirts, near the present corner of Bay and Grenville streets.

After only three years in Toronto the capital returned to Quebec where it stayed until 1856. Two years later the Toronto artist Lucius O'Brien published a lithograph showing a fashionable crowd celebrating the Queen's birthday in the grounds of old Government House. Perhaps both he and the far-sighted new governor general, Sir Edmund Head, who visited Toronto on a "deliberate viceregal progress"[11] in October 1855, were anticipating the next move.

For indeed the following year the government returned to Toronto and Elmsley House was rehabilitated. Head, as an amateur of architecture, was on hand not only to approve the Norman design of the new University of Toronto building (now University College) but to persuade the authorities to make changes in order to save a noble tree that stood on the site.[12]

But in 1859, when the government returned to Quebec for the second and last time, Elmsley again lay empty. It was still intact in September 1860, when Head entertained the Prince of Wales at a luncheon, and the Prince held a levée just after the unfortunate incident caused by the Orangemen's attempt to oblige him to walk under their arch. But the house was soon given over to the army, which occupied it until it burnt down in 1862.

Franz Winterhalter: Edward VII as Prince of Wales, 1859.

A Victorian Mansion

In 1866 in Toronto, in anticipation of the confederation of the provinces of British North America and the creation of the province of Ontario, preparations were under way for a lieutenant governor's residence. Thomas Gundry and Henry Langley, the designers of many important buildings in Toronto, were chosen to draw up the plans. But construction was delayed until 1868, and in the interval the first two lieutenant governors, Sir Henry Stistead and Sir William How-

land, were obliged to receive visitors in their own houses. The most notable visit came in the latter's time in 1869: that of the young Prince Arthur, a future occupant of Rideau Hall, who was accompanied by the governor general of that day, Lord Lisgar. It was not until June 1870 that Howland, the American-born Father of Confederation, could move into the new Government House.

Over the preceding thirty years the western half of the old province of Canada had profited from a great wave of immigrants from the British Isles and its

Government House, Toronto.
Photograph c.1890.

population had risen dramatically. Cities had sprung up in response to the development of industry, trade and communications. Toronto had become an important centre, and the new Government House[13] was conceived of as an expression of the prosperity and dignity of the capital of Ontario. But in spite of its professed loyalty to British institutions the city always kept a close eye on the neighbouring United States. Thus, as Langley explained, the building was "designed in the modern French style of architecture, which has been adopted largely in American cities".[14] This Second

The Coachmen of Government House, Toronto. Photograph c.1910.

Government House, Toronto: the Entrance Hall. Photograph c.1903-8.

Empire style, itself harking back to seventeenth-century France, was intended to supply the elegance and cosmopolitanism lacking in the New World.

Accordingly, on the site of Elmsley House, there rose a red-brick building trimmed with Ohio stone. (Some of the decorative details were executed in galvanized iron painted to simulate stone, for it was also characteristic of the age to get as much as possible for the money.) The building displayed all the fashionable exterior trappings: the high, narrow windows with segmental arches, the mansard roof with showy dormers, a *porte-cochère* resting on clustered columns, and a tower with filigree iron cresting. The gardens were laid out in what one now thinks of as "municipal" beds, and elsewhere in the grounds were a gatehouse, coach house and gardener's cottage.

Indoors, the principal rooms on the ground floor were grouped round a spacious hall with a dado, top-heavy door frames and Minton floor tiles. At the far end of the hall was a massive stair with ornate newels

Government House, Toronto: the Drawing Room. Photograph c.1903-8.

and heavy balusters, all "grained" to imitate fine woods. On the landing an arched window filled with stained glass by Joseph McCausland (1829-after 1885) shed a dim light on the hall below. On the south side of the house, with views over the gardens and Lake Ontario, was the state drawing room giving on to a shallow veranda. It was flanked by a reception room (on the east) and another drawing room which connected with the greenhouse. The west side of the house was occupied by a large ballroom, and the north-west corner by the dining room. The north-east

corner housed the lieutenant governor's offices. Throughout, the ceilings were adorned with elaborate plaster flowers from which hung glass gasoliers; and the characteristic marble fireplaces of the period abounded. A service wing attached to the north side of the house contained kitchens, pantries and a laundry.

Upstairs, the principal bedrooms and dressing rooms faced the lake, the rest of the floor being taken up by guest bedrooms. On the second floor were seven more bedrooms, a smoking room and a second billiards room. Heating was by radiators downstairs and hot-air registers upstairs.

The furnishings included ornate Rococo Revival pieces purchased from the Toronto cabinetmakers Jacques and Jay for $14,384:

> *In the hall:* a writing-table, hall chairs, a settee, a grandfather's clock and the portraits of past governors commissioned from the painter George Theodore Berthon by John Beverley Robinson.
> *In the drawing room:* two stuffed walnut sofas with silk covers, an ottoman, easy chairs, inlaid fancy round tables, a gilt mantel mirror,* gilt window cornices, silk curtains, a Wilton carpet, gilt candelabra and a French clock.
> *In the reception room:* couches, fancy tables and velvet and lace curtains.
> *In the small drawing room:* a couch, easy chairs and an inlaid cabinet.
> *In the state dining room:* a telescope table with fourteen leaves, oak chairs with morocco covers, an oak sideboard with plate-glass back, green curtains with gold borders and a Brussels carpet.
> *In the ballroom:* five settees, five large mirrors and a quantity of ballroom chairs.
> *In the bedrooms:* "French" bedsteads, one walnut half-tester bed, a cheval pedestal dressing-table, winged

Now in the Lieutenant Governor's suite of rooms in the Legislative Building.

Government House, Toronto: the Lieutenant Governor's Study. Photograph c.1903-8.

wardrobes, stuffed chairs and brocade dimity curtains. *In the pantries:* twenty dozen each "best" sets of Limoges porcelain and gold-and-white china, and glassware engraved with the provincial arms.[15]

In the early years various things went wrong with the house.[16] In 1871 Lady Macdonald, one of the earlier guests, was nearly asphyxiated by a leaky gas jet. There were leaks in the roof, rats in the cellar, drains that gave off bad smells and trouble with the water supply. But in spite of all, the entertaining was never-ending. Grand Duke Alexis, son of the liberator Tsar Alexander II, stopped over on his transcontinental tour of 1871. Lord and Lady Dufferin, constantly on the move, were entertained on several occasions at luncheon, tea, dinner, balls with special illuminations and at skating parties.[17] On the first visit of the Marquess of Lorne and Princess Louise, which took place in September 1879 during Donald Alexander Macdonald's term, the royal standard flew over the house, which by night was lit by hundreds of tiny gas jets. Oscar Wilde, in Toronto during his lecture tour of 1882, was accorded a ball by the Robinsons.

Grandest of all was the visit of the Duke and Duchess of York in 1901, in Sir Oliver Mowat's period as lieutenant governor. The royal couple arrived in an October rainstorm and were driven past an illuminated City Hall and on to Government House to the strains of the Hallelujah Chorus. At the State dinner were the prime minister Sir Wilfrid Laurier, the premier of Ontario George William Ross, the Ontario justices and members of the Osler, Gooderham, Denison, Cox and Gzowski families. At a command performance in Massey Hall the star performer was the French operatic soprano Emma Calvé, and the programme, so typical of its period, consisted of short pieces by Bizet, Massenet, Meyerbeer, Fauré, Chaminade, Gounod, Schumann and Delibes. A regatta in the harbour, a lacrosse match and visits to the University, Osgoode

Government House, Toronto, showing Illuminations for the Visit of Lord Lorne and Princess Louise, 1879.

Hall and the hospitals filled the rest of the busy schedule of activities.[18]

On the other side of the ledger were the periodic complaints made in the Legislature, particularly during periods of economic stress, of the cost of maintaining

Visit of the Duke and Duchess of Cornwall and York to Government House, Toronto, 1901. In foreground, at left: Lord and Lady Minto; centre, Sir Oliver Mowat; at right, Duke and Duchess of York.

the house. In 1884 the Revd Charles Mulvaney, author of *Toronto, Past and Present*, voiced populist sentiments that were to be echoed from time to time in years to come:

> Government House is the residence of the Hon. Beverly Robinson, at present nesting in the last year of his term of office as Lieutenant-Governor. The gardens surrounding the house are among the most beautiful in Toronto, and complaint has often been made by the independent city journals that the people should be allowed to look upon the grounds which are supported out of taxes which they pay. The apartments . . . are well and elegantly proportioned, and if ever the conviction gains ground with the taxpayers of Ontario that a grievance which costs them $50,000 a year had better be abolished, this sumptuous edifice, the people's property as it is, built and maintained by the taxpayer, would serve admirably for a State Hall or People's Palace. Still better, it might be converted into a public library and industrial museum, the grounds, now selfishly appropriated by sinecure officialdom, being utilized as a park, free forever to all our citizens.[19]

Government House Grounds, Toronto. Photograph c.1912.

In 1887 a member of the Conservative opposition in the Legislature declared that "The attempt to keep up in this city a little court mimicking Royalty was absurd. . . . The attempt to keep up the tawdry tinsel of Royalty was an insult to the intelligence of the people".[20] But the Liberal government of the day supported the cause of Government House and kept it going. In 1894-5 further motions to abolish the house were defeated, but the Opposition was then powerful enough to cause the government to appoint a select committee to look into the matter.[21] Two former lieutenant governors, Sir William Howland and John Beverley Robinson, were called to testify. It is interesting to note that an important part of their defence of the house was concerned with the American visitors, from business tycoons to labour leaders, who had been

Prince Arthur of Connaught with Sir John Eaton in the latter's car in Government House Grounds, Toronto. Photograph 1906.

so favourably impressed with the hospitality extended to them that they went home in a mood to foster American investment and good labour relations in Ontario.[22]

And so Government House weathered the storm. All the governors general of Canada arrived in their turn. Lady Aberdeen took advantage of many official visits with her husband to organize her National Council of Women. By 1897 it became apparent that Lady Kirkpatrick, the wife of the lieutenant governor of that day and a member of a Conservative family who sided with the Aberdeens' enemy the elder Sir Charles Tupper, had had enough of these visits. But Lord and Lady Aberdeen brazened out the opposition and took over Government House as a base for their own entertainments. These latter culminated in the lavish Victorian Era Ball at the Armouries, to which all Toronto society were drawn willy-nilly. There were receptions and dinners galore in the house. "Government House," wrote Lady Aberdeen, "lends itself so splendidly to entertaining."[23] Under less constraint were the Lieutenant Governor's own receptions for such august bodies as the British Association for the Advancement of Science, and for the visit of Prince Arthur, Duke of Connaught, in 1906.

In the early part of the twentieth century, with the great expansion of Toronto, and particularly with the move of Upper Canada College from King Street to

Farewell to Government House: the Last State Dinner, 29 April 1912.

the northern part of the city, Government House was left as a green island in a sea of office buildings, warehouses and railway yards. By 1910 this encroachment had made life so uncomfortable that the property was sold to the Canadian Pacific Railway. When the farewell dinner and ball were held in the old house by Sir John Gibson in April 1912, preparations were already being made for a new house. The old historic site was cleared later that same year. After a variety of uses in the intervening years, it is now occupied by office buildings, a housing complex and the Roy Thompson concert hall.

Chorley Park, Toronto.

Chorley Park

Toronto was now entering upon her "imperial" period, in which she displayed herself not only to the rest of Canada, as her market, but to the British Empire and the United States, as sources of investment in Ontario. At one and the same time her hotels and commercial buildings modelled themselves on their American counterparts while proclaiming themselves the largest in the Empire. The new Government House of 1912–15[24] inevitably partook of the same spirit. If the buildings of the Canadian National Exhibition emulated the Roman splendours of the World's Columbian Exposition of 1893 in Chicago, the new Government House was clothed in the romantic attire of the "Château" style of the railway hotels of Canada, a style of elegance and refinement which was derived from Richard Morris Hunt's design for the Vanderbilt mansion in New York.

An architectural competition was launched in 1910 for a building intended for a site in Bloor Street. But as has so often been the case in such competitons, the issue became confused. Out of the twelve designs submitted, the judges chose one in the French Renaissance style by G.W. King as the "winner" and another in "Anglo-French eighteenth-century classic" by John M. Lyle as the "best". In the end the Public Works architect Frank R. Heakes advised against the adoption of either design and produced one of his own which combined the exterior of the first with the interior of the second.[25]

The site too was changed, from Bloor Street to a fourteen-acre estate on the Rosedale Ravine, in the best residential district of Toronto. It bore the name of Chorley Park, after the Lancashire birthplace of its original owner. Here the construction of a very large house, which was eventually to cost more than two-and-a-half million dollars, was begun in 1912 and completed in time for Sir John Hendrie to move into it late in December 1915. In the interval both Hendrie and his predecessor Sir John Gibson had resided at Pendarvis, a house of 1860 by Frederick Cumberland, which is now part of the University of Toronto.

Chorley Park[26] exhibited in the extreme the picturesque silhouette of the Château style. Each of the three grey-stone pavilions on its main front — a central block with flanking wings — was covered with a steep, red-tiled pavilion roof into which were set dormers with ornate pediments. Each corner sported a turret. At the entrance was a commodious *porte-cochère* above which rose a François-Premier façade to the full height of the house. At the back were lower wings containing ballroom, greenhouses and service quarters.

:: New Government House ::
:: : Rosedale Toronto : ::

· Tennis Lawn ·

· Upper Terrace ·

Ball Rm

Kitchen

Palm Room

Corridor

Parquet

Serving Double

Private Dining Rm

Corridor

Rose Garden

Living Rm

Terrace   State Dining Room

Hall

Writing Rm

Corridor   *Corridor*

Secretary Waiting Rm   Entrance Hall   Reception Rm   Drawing Rm

Governor's Rm

Main Entrance

Porte Cochère

Main   Drive

· Walk ·

:: Ground Floor Plan ::

Chorley Park, Toronto: Plan of the Ground Floor.

Chorley Park, Toronto: the Drawing Room. From a half-tone in Construction.

The front was approached by a curving drive from the gatehouse to an outer court (with the fountain from old Government House) and then over a bridge over the ravine to a circular inner court which in turn bridged a path leading to gardens on a lower level. The grounds were designed by the New York garden architect C.W. Leavitt who, because of local pressures, was replaced by the Toronto firm of Dunnington-Grubb. There were balustraded terraces, a pond and a profusion of shrubs and garden ornaments.

On the interior, the main entrance opened into a marble atrium of Louis-Seize design, rising to a domed skylight at the top of the house. Off this court, on the ground floor, the lofty state rooms displayed a variety of styles. The drawing room was "Adam", though with a French fireplace; the dining room was "Jacobean" with a coffered ceiling; the reception room and writing room were Louis-Seize. The ballroom with a balcony was of monumental proportions and had a palm room attached to it as an anteroom to the greenhouses. The lieutenant governor's offices were also on this floor, as were a private dining room and, at the rear, the service quarters. From the court a great stair in marble and bronze was divided at a landing, off which was the billiards room. On the first floor were the grand principal bedrooms: the Royal Suite and the lieutenant governor's chambers. Here and on the second floor were the twenty-two guest bedrooms.

In the grounds, besides the gatehouse, there were garage, stables, gardeners' and coachmen's cottages, an ice plant and tennis courts. Chorley Park was easily Canada's most splendid Government House.

The furnishings, largely purchased from Eaton's department store, consisted for the most part of reproductions of period pieces. The following is a partial list:

In the court: carved oak tables, chairs and mirrors in Charles II style.
In the drawing room: rosewood Louis-Seize sofas and chairs,* a rosewood Chippendale console table and chairs* and (evidently) a few Victorian sofas and chairs covered in silver and black, from old Government House.
In the dining room: a "Jacobean" table with spiral legs* and sixty chairs.
In the reception room: two Louis-Seize mantel clocks.
In the bedrooms: a mahogany Chippendale "set" in the Royal Suite and painted furniture in other rooms.
In the pantries: the "best" gold-and-white set of Limoges and other china by Copeland and Spode.[27]

Chief among Sir John Hendrie's first visitors during the First World War was the Governor General, the Duke of Devonshire, who during his stay at Government House gave royal assent to the Conscription Act of 1917. Two years later, just after the war, the Prince of Wales was given a popular idol's welcome in Toronto; but in the photographs taken at Chorley Park the slender young Prince looks ill at ease among the top-hatted dignitaries. He returned several times, once in Henry Cockshutt's time and again in W.D. Ross's, along with his brother Prince George on the occasion of the Diamond Jubilee of Confederation.

Besides the governors general in their turn — Lord Byng, Lord Willingdon, Lord Bessborough and Lord Tweedsmuir — came a procession of the Canadian leaders of the twenties and thirties, including Sir Charles Fitzpatrick, Lieutenant Governor of Quebec, and his premier Louis-Alexandre Taschereau, on a

Starred items are now in the Lieutenant Governor's suite in the Legislative Building.

Chorley Park, Toronto: the Entrance Hall. From a half-tone in Construction.

126

Visit of the Duke and Duchess of Devonshire to Chorley Park, Toronto, 1917. Second from left, Lady Maud Cavendish; Lady Hendrie; Duke of Devonshire; Duchess of Devonshire; Sir John Hendrie (Lieutenant Governor); Miss Enid Hendrie.

mission of *bon accord* with Ontario. Foreign royalty were represented by Queen Marie of Romania, the great beauty of her day; British political figures by Sir Austen Chamberlain, David Lloyd George, Stanley Baldwin, Ramsay MacDonald and Winston Churchill; and the gentler pursuits by Sir Henry Newbolt the poet and Lord Baden-Powell the founder of Scouting. Most of these visits took place during Cockshutt's term from 1921 to 1926.

The glory of Chorley Park was quickly past. Only five lieutenant governors lived there, holding their traditional levées, Legislative dinners, charity balls, garden parties, receptions and gatherings of young

Visit of the Prince of Wales to Chorley Park, 1919. At left, Prince of Wales and Sir John Hendrie.

people. Then the axe fell.[28] In the depression election campaign of 1934 the unstable Liberal leader Mitchell Hepburn — in order to win the support of the third party, the United Farmers of Ontario, and to retain that of Joseph Atkinson, the anti-monarchist publisher of the Toronto *Star*[29] — attacked Government House as "a haven for broken-down English aristocrats who should be paying for their rooms at the hotels".[30] Hepburn won the election and while commending Dr Herbert Bruce, the lieutenant governor, for refusing to sign the lame-duck orders-in-council of the outgoing Conservative government, announced his intention of closing the house at the end of Dr Bruce's term. There was a flurry in the press, with attacks on the premier as being anti-British in King George V's jubilee year and outcries from patriotic groups like the United Empire Loyalists.[31] The real reason for the closing of Chorley Park in 1937 was, however, Hepburn's petty squabble with the prime minister, Mackenzie King, over federal appointments in Ontario.

At Government House, Toronto, 1927: Lord and Lady Willingdon with the Lieutenant Governor of Ontario and Mrs W.D. Ross; at R. the Hon. Inigo Freeman-Thomas and his wife.

His Honour Lincoln Alexander,
Lieutenant Governor of Ontario.
Photograph 1986.

The great house was the scene of an auction sale in June 1938, at which two thousand items of furnishings fetched the paltry sum of $18,000, the last item to come on the block being the watchman's clock. After standing idle for several years the building was leased for use as a military hospital during the Second World War. Beginning in 1953, it became in succession a training base for Reserve Army units, a Mounted Police headquarters and a haven for Hungarian refugees. Finally, after being bought by the city of Toronto for a mere $100,000, it was ignominiously demolished in 1961. The property became a public park with nothing but the little bridge in the forecourt to remind the visitor of the glories of Chorley Park.

Meanwhile, lacking an official residence, the lieutenant governors of Ontario made do with their own houses and with a limited space for offices and receptions in a wing of the Legislative Building. Thus in 1939 there was no place in which to accommodate King George VI and Queen Elizabeth, who were obliged to stay aboard their train. Several attempts in the intervening years to provide a new Government House have failed for one reason or another.

And so, in the era of her greatest prosperity, Canada's richest province has had no official residence. The lack of it has not, however, prevented such vigorous incumbents of the office as Pauline McGibbon in the period from 1974 to 1980, John B. Aird from 1980 to 1985, or the present lieutenant governor, Lincoln Alexander, from undertaking the most energetic programmes in history throughout the province. Under Mrs McGibbon in 1980, a movement was set afoot to collect and borrow period furniture and other works of art for the present quarters. Here also, to remind the visitor of past history, are assorted pieces from two former Government Houses and the portraits of all former governors and lieutenant governors.[32]

W.D. Ross with guests at a Garden
Party, c.1927-32.

Lieutenant Governors of Upper Canada 1792-1841

John Graves Simcoe (1752-1806)	1792-1799
Peter Hunter (1746-1805)	1799-1805
Francis Gore (1769-1852)	1806-1818
Sir Peregrine Maitland (1777-1854)	1818-1828
Sir John Colborne, later 1st Baron Seaton (1778-1863)	1828-1835
Sir Francis Bond Head, Bt (1793-1863)	1835-1838
Sir George Arthur (1784-1854)	1838-1841

Lieutenant Governors of the Province of Ontario 1867-

Sir Henry William Stistead (1817-1875)	1867-1868
Sir William Pearce Howland (1811-1907)	1868-1873
John Willoughby Crawford (1817-1875)	1873-1875
Donald Alexander Macdonald (1817-1896)	1875-1880
John Beverley Robinson (1821-1896)	1880-1887
Sir Alexander Campbell (1822-1892)	1887-1892
Sir George Airey Kirkpatrick (1841-1899)	1892-1897
Sir Oliver Mowat (1820-1903)	1897-1903
Sir William Mortimer Clark	1903-1908
Sir John Morison Gibson (1842-1929)	1908-1914
Sir John Strathearn Hendrie (1857-1923)	1914-1919
Lionel Herbert Clarke (1859-1921)	1919-1921
Henry Cockshutt (1868-1944)	1921-1926
William Donald Ross (1869-1947)	1926-1932
Herbert Alexander Bruce (1868-1963)	1932-1937
Albert Matthews (1873-1949)	1937-1946
Ray Lawson (1886-	1946-1952
Louis Orville Breithaupt (1890-1960)	1952-1957
John Keiller MacKay (1888-1970)	1957-1963
William Earl Rowe (1894-	1963-1968
William Ross MacDonald	1968-1974
Pauline Emily McGibbon (1910-	1974-1980
John Black Aird (1923-	1980-1985
Lincoln Alexander (1922-	1985

British Columbia

*J*osephine Crease: Government
House, Victoria. Water colour, 1880.

The Beginnings: Victoria and New Westminster

Though Sir Francis Drake seems to have sighted Vancouver Island on his voyage of 1579, and though the Spanish had sailed along the north-west coast in 1774-5, James Cook was the first to make a recorded landing in what is now British Columbia. This took place at Nootka Sound in 1778, while he was on his way to the Bering Sea. When his account of trading with the Indians was published in 1784, British ships began to arrive. The Spanish seized some of these, but the British government made such strenuous complaints that Spain was obliged to open the region to all comers. In 1792 Captain George Vancouver began his survey of the coast, and the following year Alexander Mackenzie of the North West Company reached the Pacific overland from Canada. In the first decade of the nineteenth century two other representatives of the Company founded trading posts: Simon Fraser on the river which bears his name, and David Thomson on the Columbia.

By 1821 the North West Company had amalgamated with the Hudson's Bay Company, which henceforth operated along the coast from California to Russian Alaska. Meanwhile American settlers had begun to arrive in the Oregon country; and in 1843 the Hudson's Bay Company, in anticipation of the boundary settlement of 1845, had founded Fort Victoria on Vancouver Island. Eventually it moved its headquarters there from Fort Vancouver at the mouth of the Columbia.

In 1849 the British government granted Vancouver Island to the Company but appointed its own governor in the person of Richard Blanshard, a young English barrister. He arrived in Victoria in March 1850; and James Douglas, head of the Company's operations on the coast, was directed to build a house for him.

This first Government House[1] was a small shingled cottage near the fort, on the site of the present post office at the corner of Government and Yates streets. As Douglas reported to headquarters in London in September 1850, there had been unavoidable delays, and it had been impossible to keep pace with Blanshard's demands; but

> The House is nearly finished and he will soon move into it; so that there will be an end of trouble, from that source.
> The size of the Governor's House is 40x20 ft, with a Kitchen 18x12 feet attached, and a house of 24x18 feet for his servants. The house is ceiled and painted inside. It has a neat appearance, and is, on the whole the best finished building in Oregon.

The Governor, for his part, added an extension to the house. Douglas noted in April 1851 that "though of moderate size, [it] is comfortable, and has a very neat and respectable appearance".[2]

Ill, and frustrated by his relations with the Company, Blanshard resigned his post and left the colony in September 1851. Douglas then became governor and used the house as his office while living in his own house on the south shore of James Bay.

In 1858 the discovery of gold on the Fraser River brought a rush of American prospectors to the mainland. In order to secure the British claim to the territory north of the 49th Parallel, the Colonial Office in London created a second Crown Colony, British Columbia, with Douglas also as its governor. The Government House for this colony was built in 1862 on the banks of the Fraser at New Westminster. It stood within the Royal Engineers' camp and was occupied by their colonel, Richard Moody, who was commissioner of lands and held a dormant commission as lieutenant governor under Douglas. A large wooden cottage of distinctly *québécois* design, it had a steep roof with dormers, tall French windows and flaring eaves extending over both sides. Douglas had admired

How We Appeared on Arrival in B.C., 1864; *Frederick Seymour (seated) with his staff on the veranda of Government House, New Westminster.*

the plans for it, which had been drawn up by John Clayton White (d. 1907), a corporal in the Engineers, as "decidedly pretty and the arrangement comfortable".[3] It had three rooms on the ground floor and three bedrooms and a sitting room upstairs.

Douglas, now Sir James, moved into the house at New Westminster in March 1864. Only weeks before his retirement that same year he held a reception to celebrate the birth of the Prince of Wales's first son, Prince Albert, Duke of Clarence.

After Douglas's retirement each colony was given its own governor. To the mainland, in April 1864, came Frederick Seymour, formerly governor of British Honduras. At once he built a new wing to his house. This pretty addition, also designed by Corporal White, with a large bay window and a little balcony off the first floor and an iron-crested tower, stood at right angles to the house. It contained the "magnificent lofty ballroom" in which the Governor held his first ball in November. The Victoria *Colonist* reported that some two hundred guests came, some of them by ship from Victoria. Dancing commenced at nine and continued until midnight. Then "the doors of the supper room were thrown open disclosing one of the most elegant and tastefully arranged tables that we have seen at any private entertainment". Dancing resumed and went on until nearly four o'clock in the morning, when the band played the National Anthem and "many voices joined to do homage to England's Queen".[4]

In 1866 Seymour became governor of the united colonies; and when the capital was moved to Victoria in 1868, he was loath to leave his house in New Westminster. Occupied by Canadian Pacific engineers from 1881 to 1883, it was falling into disrepair when Sir John and Lady Macdonald were entertained there in 1886. Eventually it became a part of the provincial penitentiary property and was demolished in 1889 to make way for the warden's house.

John Clayton White: Government House, New Westminster. Water colour, 1866.

Government House, Victoria (Cary Castle): the East Front. Photograph c.1860.

Cary Castle

Meanwhile, in Victoria, the handsome and courtly Arthur Kennedy, until recently governor of Western Australia, had been appointed to Vancouver Island. On his arrival in March 1864 he leased Joseph Trutch's house Fairfield during its owner's absence from Victoria. But when Trutch returned in the spring of 1865, and while the Assembly cavilled at providing him with a house, he took matters into his own hands and bought one on his own responsibility. In it he held his first ball in October of the same year. It was perhaps the spirit of Kennedy's generous entertaining that led one young man to serenade the Governor's daughter outside the house one evening and to be arrested for this crime.

The house in question was "Cary Castle",[5] a small stone villa named for its builder, the eccentric attorney-general, George Cary. He had built it a year after arriving in the colony in 1859. (According to some sources it had been begun by someone else in the early 1850s but was rebuilt by Cary after a fire.) Cary's architect was Frederick Walter Green (d. 1877) who later became surveyor of Victoria. It was presumably he who (in 1860) was responsible for the crenellated walls and round tower and the arched *porte-cochère*. The earliest photographs show a rather truncated building, suggesting that it had been left unfinished when Cary lost it in a foreclosure in 1862. By the time of Kennedy's purchase it belonged to a Mrs John Miles, who named it Stoneleigh and added some property to the grounds.

The best feature of Cary Castle was its site on a rocky eminence with a superb view across the Strait of Juan de Fuca to the Olympic Range in the distance. Its worst features were that it had no water supply and was cold and draughty in winter; but such was the price to be paid for a romantic site and a Border

Government House, Victoria (Cary Castle): the North Front, the Ballroom at right. Photograph c.1865.

castle out of the novels of Sir Walter Scott. The Assembly, having had its hand forced, now agreed to make what additions to the house as were necessary for its use as an official residence. These additions were designed by John Wright (1830–1915), the Scottish-born architect of Italianate villas in Victoria.

Only a portion of the plans was realized during Kennedy's short reign. By October 1865 a large ballroom had lengthened the north (or entrance) front towards the west; and a new range of buildings along the back had provided a much-needed living room downstairs. The *porte-cochère* was walled in to form a vestibule for the entrance hall. For reasons of economy the new work was carried out in frame construction, with roughcast exterior surfaces. Indoors, the new ballroom attracted the most attention in its day, as the first of its kind for official entertaining:

> The ballroom, a fine lofty and well ventilated apartment, 50x25x23 feet [had] a handsomely ornamented ceiling, from which were suspended three splendid chandeliers that diffused a brilliant light over the scene.

Josephine Crease: the Billiard Room, Government House, Victoria. Water colour, 1880.

On one side of the room are two elegant mantel pieces, one bearing the Colonial and the other the Royal Arms, which were much admired.[6]

In 1866 Kennedy held several more balls in the house before his departure was announced in October. In that month, in Government House, he auctioned off his personal possessions including a grand piano and two carriages.

Seymour, who became governor of the united colony of British Columbia after its proclamation in November 1866, had two Government Houses. He much preferred his "cottage without pretensions on the Banks of the Fraser", but in 1868, when the capital was fixed at Victoria, he was obliged to make do with the bare, unfurnished Cary Castle, which he regarded as "singularly unattractive",[7] and which was already in need of repairs because of its exposure to the elements and the flimsiness of the additions of 1865.

The remainder of Wright's architectural proposals for Government House were undertaken at once. A new "Gothic" roof (really a Second Empire pavilion with dormers) now capped the original house. The original stonework was now plastered over to match the new parts. The east wing was enlarged by the addition of two single-storeyed pavilions, the one with a skylight serving as a billiards room opening into the drawing room, the other forming a dining room. Each pavilion was given a bay window of three arched lights. Offices for the governor were added at the rear and a greenhouse and croquet lawn were provided in the grounds. In the interior, the drawing room and "little round room" in the tower were painted in white and gold. Furniture was moved from New Westminster, and two glass chandeliers were ordered from England. Most of this work was completed in a great hurry in time for Seymour's official arrival in his capital in May 1868. Afterwards a guard house was built and a telegraph line from town was extended to the house.

After Seymour's sudden death at Bella Coola in June 1869, and the State funeral, his successor Anthony Musgrave, previously governor of Newfoundland, inherited the refurbished house. His term was plagued by ill-health and bad luck. The only Queen's Birthday ball he and his new wife (a daughter of the American cable magnate Cyrus Field) held was marred by a small fire in the ballroom. But there were more serious concerns. His two-year period in office was one of sore vexation over the delay in granting full responsible government to the colony and of angry

The Guard House, Government House Grounds, Victoria. Photograph c.1868.

threats of annexation to the United States. The subsequent negotiations with Canada led to British Columbia's entry into Confederation in 1871, with a pledge on the part of Macdonald's Conservatives to complete a transcontinental railway within ten years.

Joseph Trutch, one of the chief negotiators of Confederation, was chosen by Macdonald as first lieutenant governor of the province of British Columbia. He found Government House once more to be in need of repairs. These were delayed until the province's responsibility in the matter had been determined, but by 1873 all was complete and the house had been enlarged by a further extension across the back. Now

in its final form, it was used to full advantage in a flurry of entertaining. This was, however, short-lived because of the limitations of Trutch's salary and the renewal of anti-Confederation sentiment.

The lieutenant governor who succeeded him found himself in a yet more difficult situation. Albert Richards, a former federal legal adviser to the province, was appointed in 1876 by Mackenzie's Liberals in Ottawa during a period of economic depression and of delays in building the railway. Attention was temporarily deflected from Richards at the outset of his term by the arrival of the Governor General, Lord Dufferin. It was Dufferin, not Richards, who lived in Government House and received the angry delegations

Chinese servants at Government House, Victoria. Photograph c.1876.

threatening secession. As the Governor General pre-pared his great "Columbia Speech", in which he took it upon himself to explain federal government policy and thus got himself into serious trouble with his ministers, his wife was savouring the life in Cary Castle.[8] Though her husband reported that Richards was denounced locally as a "carpet bagger",[9] she found his house "very nice and comfortable" in spite of the lack of water ("Every Drop . . . has to be brought in barrels") and of such eccentricities as prisoners in chains working in the grounds and an ugly old Chinese cook with a child bride. In spite of all, the Dufferins managed to hold a variety of entertainments culminating in a grand ball:

> At seven we had a merry little dinner in a small room. There was a rumor that the great Ah Sâm [the cook]

was drunk, and that the supper would be very bad; but the dinner was all right, so we felt some hope. The guests were invited at 8:30, and soon after nine D. and I came down to open the ball. The room is a very nice one, and we had all the windows taken out, and a sort of corridor tent of canvas, lined with flags, put up the whole way round the outside, which added greatly to the available space . . . . We all danced from 9:30 till three without interruption, and as fathers, mothers, daughters, and sons are all equally dancing-mad here, and as we had a great number of naval officers, and were in ourselves an element of novelty among the Victorians, and they were new to us, there was a great deal of spirit in the ball.[10]

Once the visit was over, and Richards installed in the house, the wrath of the provincial government fell

Government House, Victoria (Cary Castle) from the North-west.

Government House, Victoria (Cary Castle): the Drawing Room looking into the Ballroom.

on him. He was threatened with the "unroofing" of Government House, and in 1877-8 he saw his allowances for water and fuel cut off. He in turn threatened to abandon the house "to the bats and owls". Yet in the midst of his troubles he held an evening of theatricals. "The ball room," reported the *Colonist*, "was divided off and a stage erected at the west end making a perfect little *bijou* of a theatre."[11] Supper and dancing followed. This took place in April 1877. As the situation worsened Government House virtually closed its doors, though in 1879 the government was obliged to make emergency repairs to avoid irreparable damage.

More favourable were the times, and more congenial the next lieutenant governor. Clement Cornwall was a gentleman rancher who had introduced riding to hounds on his mainland estate. When he assumed office in 1881 extensive repairs were made to the house and new furnishings were bought. The inventories of

Government House, Victoria (Cary Castle): the Hall and Stair. Photograph c.1880.

142

the period list such items of Victoriana as the following:

> *In the hall:* four stained benches and a table, a marble-topped table and two pairs of antlers.
> *In the ballroom:* "black rugs" (imitation bear skins) and a china "moderator" lamp.
> *In the dining room:* an extension oak table, eighteen carved oak chairs covered in green plush and pictures of the Royal Family.
> *In the lieutenant governor's study:* a carved oak desk, a telephone and a copying press.
> *In the bedrooms:* iron bedsteads with palliasses and bolsters, wardrobes, marble-topped tables, hip-baths, chintz-covered furniture and carpet over oilcloth. The Royal Bedroom had a "canopy brass double bedstead", a pier-glass and chintz curtains.[12]

It was in Cornwall's term, in September 1882, that the first visit of a member of the Royal Family took place.[13] By then the Canadian Pacific was under construction, and the arrival of the Governor General, Lord Lorne, and his handsome wife Princess Louise stirred up a carnival spirit in Victoria. Crowds, welcome arches, parades of soldiers and fire-engines, Chinese bands, a fusillade of flowers, and children's choirs greeted them along their way from the ship to Government House. To the Princess, who sketched Government House and its famous view, the place seemed "halfway between Heaven and Balmoral".[14] A series of elaborate entertainments made of the occasion a delayed celebration of British Columbia's entry into Confederation.

Lord Lansdowne ("If I had to live on this continent I should pitch my tent here")[15] paid his official visit to Victoria in 1885, shortly before the first train arrived on the coast. When the railway made

Princess Louise: Mount Baker from Government House, Victoria. Water colour, 1882.

travelling easier from eastern Canada, the visits of governors general became more frequent, Lord and Lady Stanley came in the new viceregal railway carriage *Victoria* in 1889. The Aberdeens came first in 1895, in Edgar Dewdney's period as lieutenant governor, with the energetic Lady Aberdeen occupying most of her time as usual in forming a Local Council of Women. The following year they appropriated Government House for themselves and kept everyone busy: "We shall be very happy here," wrote Lady Aberdeen, "the house is roomy and comfortable."[16] Royalty was represented by Prince Arthur who stopped on his way home from India in 1890, and politics by Sir John A. Macdonald who came during an election campaign in 1886. Two years later Lady Macdonald was received by Hugh Nelson, the lieutenant governor, at a garden party in her honour. Life in the house was accordingly enlivened with such Victorian pastimes as, on one occasion, a "Cinderella ball".

Cary Castle was, however, soon to suffer the fate of so many buildings in Canada. In May 1899, at the end of Thomas McInnes's term, the entire house except for the ballroom and some of the furniture was destroyed in a spectacular fire. This disaster, in spite of hurried preparations for a new house, left no place in 1901 in which to accommodate the grandest of all visitors to date, the Duke and Duchess of Cornwall and York. The royal couple were put up in the Mount Baker Hotel at Oak Bay and the State dinner was held in the Lieutenant Governor's temporary house in Moss Street.* The story is told of this dinner that an important but very old lady had an animated conversation with some young man seated next to her at table. Only afterwards was it borne in on her that he was the Prince.[17]

Gyppeswyk (1889), now a part of the Art Gallery of Victoria.

Government House twice rebuilt

The lieutenant governor at the turn of the century was well suited to his place and time. The courtly Sir Henri Joly de Lotbinière had been a Member of Parliament and, for a short period, premier of Quebec. Residing on his ancient seigniory on the St Lawrence, he had wide connections with the great world of his day. He was the presiding genius not only of the growing prosperity and importance of British Columbia but of a grander reincarnation of Cary Castle.

In the architectural competition announced in October 1900 the "winner" was the firm of Byrnes and Tait of Victoria; but in the end the commission was awarded to the city's two most creative architects. The one, Samuel Maclure (1860-1929), was the designer of many attractive private houses in the style generally referred to as "Elizabethan Vernacular", but which in actuality was compounded of elements from Norman Shaw and Charles Voysey of the Arts and Crafts Movement in England, and from H.H. Richardson's "Shingle Style" and Frank Lloyd Wright's Prairie Style in the United States. The other architect was Maclure's friend Francis Mawson Rattenbury (1867-1935), a talented Englishman who was master of many styles ranging from "Beaux-Arts" Classicism (which he had interpreted in an almost Mogul richness in the Legislative Building in Victoria) to the "Château" style of the great Empress Hotel in the same city.[18]

The exterior of the new Government House[19], with its splendid mixture of styles, appears to have been Rattenbury's contribution, as Maclure was ill at the time. The stone central block had a crenellated square tower vaguely reminiscent of Cary Castle. Flanking it on either side were more-or-less symmetrical frame wings covered with brown shingles, thus eccentrically combining Norman Shaw and H.H. Richardson. A circular corner tower gave yet another

Government House, Victoria: the West Front. Photograph c.1903.

Government House, Victoria: the Dining Room.

reminder of Cary Castle. Other wings at the back rambled picturesquely along the rock brow of the hill.

The interior was as eclectic as the exterior but had a distinction that was the product of Maclure's attention to detail. The Elizabethan, Jacobean and Georgian styles alternated in the rooms according to their functions. The drawing room was "Jacobean", with geometric plasterwork in the ceiling and pilasters, and the dining room "Tudor" with a beamed ceiling. The splendid ballroom was vaguely Georgian but also contained an elegant series of Art Nouveau ceiling frescoes representing Indian "totemic" legends and large bay windows filled with heraldic stained glass. Both these decorative features were the work of the New Westminster artist James Bloomfield (1871-1951). By 1951, unfortunately, the frescoes had come to be regarded as old-fashioned and were painted over in preparation for the visit of Princess Elizabeth and Prince Philip. In addition to the pieces saved from the fire in the old house, loads of new furniture were purchased from Staynes and Wolfe of London and other cabinetmakers, in styles appropriate to the scheme of decoration for each room. A partial list of the furnishings includes the following:

In the dining room: a "Jacobean" dining table and chairs with turned legs.
In other ground-floor rooms: an antique gate-legged table, two oak side tables, a stuffed double ottoman, stuffed lounge chairs covered with tapestry, inlaid tables, Regency chairs, screens, six wicker Derby chairs, two upholstered Buxton chairs, six oak chairs with rush seats, "painted tapestry panels" with scenes of British Columbia history, two beaten brass jardinières, two oak-and-brass palm stands, iron fire-dogs and glass electroliers.
In the bedrooms: one "double Italian brass bedstead", a dressing table with oval mirror, a "stained dull green oak suite", and flax and taffeta curtains.[20]

Joly de Lotbinière moved into the house in August 1903. Besides having had a hand in planning and furnishing the rooms he planted rows of specimen trees in the grounds. His successor James Dunsmuir

Government House, Victoria: the Ballroom.

commissioned Maclure to design a Tudor-arched *porte-cochère*. The gardens, as was appropriate in that part of Canada where the art was most highly developed, were laid out in 1908 with drives, a pond and iron fences during the term of Thomas Paterson. They were the work of the Vancouver landscape artist G.K. Maclean but were redesigned in their present form by Maclure in 1927 for Walter Nichol. The gates, installed by Paterson in 1912, incorporated bronzework by the Tiffany studio in New York.

All the established activities of an official residence — the endless round of receptions, dinners, garden parties and balls — took place on a larger scale in Cary Castle *redivivus*. The regular visits of governors general brought Lord Grey in 1906 (he thought Princess

Visit of Lord and Lady Willingdon to Government House, Victoria, 1929. Second from left: the Lieutenant Governor, R.R. Bruce; Lady Willingdon; Lord Willingdon.

Visit of the Duke and Duchess of Connaught to Government House, Victoria, 1912. Front row, left to right: Princess Patricia; Mrs Paterson; Duke of Connaught; Duchess of Connaught; the Lieutenant Governor, T.W. Paterson.

Louise might have located Government House somewhat closer to heaven than to Balmoral), the Duke of Connaught in 1912, the Duke of Devonshire in 1917 ("not a bad house but not well arranged as the best view is blocked by a back room"[21]), Lord Byng in 1924, the Willingdons in 1927, the Bessboroughs in 1932, the Tweedsmuirs in 1936, Lord Athlone and Princess Alice in 1941 and the Alexanders in 1946. The Prince of Wales stayed in the house in 1919 and 1927, the Duke of Gloucester in 1929 and King George VI

and Queen Elizabeth in 1939. Numerous over the years were the varied lesser events and entertainments.

The two wars interrupted the routine. During the First World War a mob visited Government House to threaten the wife of the lieutenant governor Sir Frank Barnard, because she was of German descent. During the Second World War the Opposition in the Legislature suggested turning the house into a home for the aged or a hospital. But it survived these crises to receive the still more numerous royal visits of the postwar

A Costume Ball at Government House, Victoria. Photograph c.1939.

*The Fire at Government House,
Victoria. Photograph 1957.*

New Government House, Victoria: the North Front. Photograph c.1985.

New Government House, Victoria: the Drawing Room. Photograph 1985.

period, especially that of Princess Elizabeth in 1951. Winston Churchill and Franklin D. Roosevelt were among the world political figures who stayed in the house.

Like its predecessor, the second Cary Castle fell prey to the flames. In April 1957 it was reduced to ruins, and the lieutenant governor of the day, Frank Ross, was obliged to live in the Empress Hotel during the British Columbia centenary celebrations of 1958.

The provincial department of Public Works set about at once building a replacement, which was finished in 1959. This, the third house on the site, took the same general lines as its predecessor. It is most commodious and comfortable even if its eclectic exterior design lacks a certain cohesion. Retaining only the *porte-cochère* of 1903, its main front employs a great variety of British Columbia materials as a surface

skin over a steel-and-concrete structure intended to withstand fire. The interiors, especially of the drawing room and dining room, are remarkably close to Maclure's original designs. The ballroom with its circular bay is of hotel size. Mr and Mrs Ross chose pieces of furniture in England and had others made in Scotland; and they inspired donations of porcelain, silver, glass and pictures.

Recent lieutenant governors, notably General George Pearkes (whose wife formed a garden of native plants), Walter Owen, Henry Bell-Irving, Robert Gordon Rogers, and the present occupant David See-Chai Lam, have all used the house to full advantage in the capital and as a base for their tireless activities throughout the province.

Government House, Victoria, is second to none in Canada today in reflecting the dignity of the Crown and the attachment of its province to the Monarchy. The recent visitors, besides all governors general since its opening in 1959, have included the Queen and Prince Philip, Prince Charles, Prince Andrew, Princess Margaret, Princess Alexandra of Kent, King Hussein of Jordan, Lord Mountbatten, Lord Montgomery, Lord Slim, General Mark Clark and Chancellor Helmut Schmidt of Germany. The general public have for many years been admitted to the gardens, and large numbers visit the house each year on organized tours.

Robert Gordon Rogers and Mrs Rogers in Government House, Victoria. Photograph 1984.

Government House Grounds, Victoria. Photograph 1985.

His Honour David See-Chai Lam in Government House, Victoria. Photograph 1988.

H.M. The Queen, with the Lieutenant Governor, John Robert Nicholson, at the State Dinner in Government House, Victoria, 1971.

Governors of Vancouver Island 1849-1866

Richard Blanshard (1817?-1894)	1849-1851
Sir James Douglas (1803-1877)	1851-1864
Sir Arthur Edward Kennedy (1810-1883)	1864-1866

Governors of British Columbia 1858-1866

Sir James Douglas (1803-1877)	1858-1864
Frederick Seymour (1820-1869)	1864-1866

Governors of British Columbia 1866-1871

Frederick Seymour (1820-1869)	1866-1869
Sir Anthony Musgrave (1828-1888)	1869-1871

Lieutenant Governors of British Columbia 1871-

Sir Joseph William Trutch (1826-1904)	1871-1876
Albert Norton Richards (1822-1897)	1876-1881
Clement Francis Cornwall (1836-1910)	1881-1887
Hugh Nelson (1836-1893)	1887-1892
Edgar Dewdney (1835-1916)	1892-1897
Thomas Robert McInnes (1840-1904)	1897-1900
Sir Henri Gustave Joly de Lotbinière (1829-1908)	1900-1906
James Dunsmuir (1851-1920)	1906-1909
Thomas William Paterson (1852-1921)	1909-1914
Sir Francis Stillman Barnard (1856-1936)	1914-1919
Edward Gawler Prior (1853-1920)	1919-1920
Walter Cameron Nichol (1866-1928)	1920-1926
Robert Randolph Bruce (1863-1942)	1926-1931
John William Fordham Johnson (1866-1938)	1931-1936
Eric Werge Hamber (1880-1960)	1936-1941
William Culham Woodward (1885-1957)	1941-1946
Charles Arthur Banks (1885-1961)	1946-1950
Clarence Wallace (1894-	1950-1955
Frank MacKenzie Ross (1891-1971)	1955-1960
George Randolph Pearkes (1888-1984)	1960-1968
John Robert Nicholson (1901-	1968-1973
Walter Stewart Owen (1904-c.1980)	1973-1978
Henry Pybus Bell-Irving (1913-	1978-1984
Robert Gordon Rogers (1919–	1984-1988
David See-Chai Lam (1923–	1988

Prairie Provinces

Manitoba
The Northwest Territories and Saskatchewan
Alberta

156

*T*he Hon. Errick Willis and Mrs
Willis beside Government House,
Winnipeg. Photograph 1960.

Manitoba

The fur trade was the motive behind the early exploration of the territory that is now Manitoba. In the seventeenth and early eighteenth centuries the English entered it from Hudson Bay and the French by canoe from the St Lawrence. By the early nineteenth century the Hudson's Bay Company had established a network of trading forts fanning out from the bay, and the North West Company, successor to the Montreal *voyageurs,* had its posts in the Red River country. The traders who settled down and married Indian wives gave rise to a Métis population in the region. In 1812 Lord Selkirk brought out a company of dispossessed Scots, along with some Swiss and French, who settled on the Red River as farmers. The numbers of Roman Catholics among them drew French-speaking missionaries from Canada, and these did much to consolidate the population into a French community. By 1821 the North West Company had been absorbed into the Hudson's Bay Company, which in 1836 reasserted its jurisdiction over the Red River settlement, appointing a governor and council from its London headquarters.

By 1840 trade had sprung up between the Red River and St Paul in American territory to the south. A decade or so later, settlers from eastern Canada,

Anonymous: Silver Heights, the Residence of Lt. Gov. Archibald. *Wood-engraving in* Canadian Illustrated News, *1871.*

attracted by the fertile land, began to drift in. These, with their traditions of a settled life, contrasted sharply with the Métis who combined agriculture with the nomadic life of the buffalo hunt. Conflict between the two groups was brought to a head by the purchase of the Hudson's Bay Company's territories in 1869 by the new nation of Canada. The English-speaking settlers generally favoured union with Canada, the Métis felt themselves a nation apart.

Thus in October 1869 the young Louis Riel set up a provisional government, seized Fort Garry at the confluence of the Red and Assiniboine rivers, and prevented the Canadian lieutenant governor, William McDougall, and his council from taking office. The Riel uprising collapsed as soon as Sir Garnet Wolseley's expedition reached Fort Garry from the east in August 1870. But the non-observance of the provisions of the Manitoba Act of 1870, admitting the new province but also providing for bilingualism, led to further disputes over language and education, which have lasted until our own day.

New waves of homesteaders arrived meanwhile to grow the wheat which the Canadian Pacific Railway, after its completion in 1886, shipped to world markets. In the twenty years after 1870 the population of the province increased rapidly, and by 1912 the extension of its territory to the present boundaries had given access to the sea through Hudson Bay. The capital, Winnipeg, which had grown up around Fort Garry, and which had only a few hundred inhabitants in 1870, became the metropolis of the west in a matter of decades. Across the Red River lay its French-speaking twin, Saint-Boniface.

The history of official residences in Winnipeg[1] began with Riel's brief occupancy of the doctor's house inside Fort Garry. But when McDougall, one of the Fathers of Confederation, was designated lieutenant governor of Manitoba and the Northwest Territories in

1870, Silver Heights, a cottage built about 1856 by a retired Hudson's Bay officer, was chosen as his residence. Situated in a grove of silver poplars on the Portage Road five miles west of the fort, it was a pretty building with a pavilion roof in the *québécois* manner, extending over a gallery at the front. But McDougall having been prevented from entering his province, the furnishings that accompanied him were marooned across the American border from Pembina.

After McDougall had been removed from office by the federal authorities, his mantle fell upon the capable shoulders of Sir Adams Archibald.* Finding Silver Heights not only in disorder but too far from his seat of government, he persuaded Ottawa to lease a house for him in Fort Garry. Silver Heights was sold in 1872 to Donald A. Smith, then chief commissioner of the Hudson's Bay Company, and later Lord Strathcona of Canadian Pacific fame.

On the first visit of a governor general to Manitoba, Smith lent the house for use as a temporary viceregal residence. Lord and Lady Dufferin, who arrived by river steamer from St Paul in August 1877, were received with great enthusiasm. Dufferin, in speeches delivered in both English and French, and particularly in his "great oration" with its "Tennysonian richness and vividness", gave Manitobans as a whole their first sense of community and of a place in Canadian life.[2] Lady Dufferin for her part described the arrival at Winnipeg and later at Silver Heights in her journal:

> We left our anchorage early in the morning, and came in sight of Fort Garry about ten o'clock. The Red River appears to divide the town in two, but we left it, and turned into the Assiniboine, round the corner of which

*Later lieutenant governor of Nova Scotia

Government House in Fort Garry,
Winnipeg. Photograph c.1880.

159

we found a wharf. We had two hours to wait before landing. Some people came aboard to see the Governor-General, and he arranged for me to start half an hour before him, and to go to the City Hall, where we ladies sat till the noise of bands and shouting announced his arrival in a carriage-and-four.

The town of Winnipeg is rapidly increasing, and today, with its decorations of transplanted trees and flags, it looked gay and pretty. A very large number of people assembled round the platform, and came along the streets with D., and some very handsome arches had

been put up. Addresses were read and answered, the soldiers inspected, and then I got with D. into the carriage, and drove to "Silver Heights", where we are to live.

It is quite five miles from town, along a prairie road, which is a little rough when the weather is dry, but which is simply impassable when there has been rain. . . .

"Our house" is a cottage, and lent to us by Mr. Donald Smith, who met us at the door, introduced us to his daughter, and showed us our accommodation. The

Government House in Fort Garry, Winnipeg. Lord and Lady Dufferin in a Carriage. Photograph 1877.

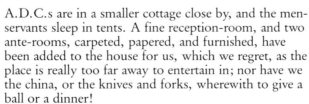

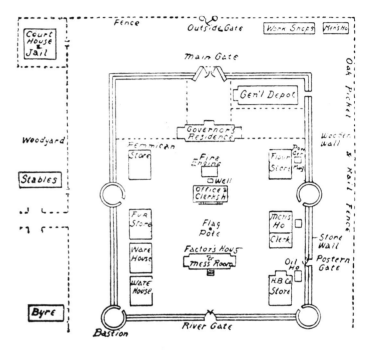

Plan of Fort Garry, c.1880.

A.D.C.s are in a smaller cottage close by, and the men-servants sleep in tents. A fine reception-room, and two ante-rooms, carpeted, papered, and furnished, have been added to the house for us, which we regret, as the place is really too far away to entertain in; nor have we the china, or the knives and forks, wherewith to give a ball or a dinner!

We are near the road, and on the other side of it is the Assiniboine River; we sat on its banks, had tea on the balcony of the house, and spent a very quiet evening.[3]

The following day they went into town to call at Government House. This was the former McTavish (or Hudson Bay) House, a large two-storeyed building just inside the main gate of the

fort, which Archibald had occupied in 1870 and where he had held his first Legislative dinner:

It was superlatively interesting. The favored of the Court, who were in juxtaposition to His Honour, wore the most recent evening dress. All Canadians, of course, dressed appropriately, but the other members wore their ordinary holiday attire, common to the country, which was in many instances, very pictur-esque. At that table was seen the broadcloth cápot of the Hudson Bay Company, with polished brass but-tons, Hudson Bay sash and moccasins; some in Scotch tweed suits; others in frock coats, and the most surprising thing was the ease of manner displayed by all. The table manners were all the most fastidious would desire, and the conversation edifying.[4]

By 1873 a third storey had been added to the house, and the whole building had been clapboarded. Some of McDougall's original furnishings, including six dining-room sofas and a bedroom set, had been retrieved and installed along with new items purchased for $5000. As described by Lady Dufferin in 1877 the house was "surrounded by a wooden palisade, and has a brick gateway, which forms a nice old-fashioned court in front".[5] On one of the Dufferins' evenings in Winnipeg a ball was held for them in Government House:

We were asked at nine o'clock, and went punctually, but "in honor of us" the other people were late, and we stood about for a long time before the dancing began.

A fine room had been put up for the occasion, and everything went off very well.
All the ladies were well dressed, and the dancing as at Ottawa or London. Six years ago, at a ball here, ladies would have come in moccasins, and danced nothing but the Red River jig. The state of life would have had some charm for us, but the change shows how rapidly the place grows, and how quickly outside ideas make their way in. The jig was danced for us; it is exactly the same as an Irish jig. The supper was good, and the table prettily decorated with flowers. The fruit had to be imported, as none grows here yet. The Roman Catholic and English bishops both came to the ball for a few minutes.[6]

But Alexander Morris, lieutenant governor during the Dufferins' visit (and founder of the University of

Old Legislative Building, Winnipeg, with Government House at left in Kennedy Street. Photograph by Gray, 1899.

Manitoba) was not so well pleased with his house. To one who had to live in it, it was an "old rambling apology for a Government House".[7] From spring well into summer it had five feet of water in the basement; and there was the irritation of having the Hudson's Bay Company still occupying a wing which they had reserved for their own use. Nevertheless Government House, under Morris's successor Joseph-Édouard Cauchon, a former Speaker of the Senate, was the scene of New Year's levées at which the Lieutenant Governor received delegations of Indians, heard their requests and smoked with them the pipe of peace. Here too he received the Marquess of Lorne on the latter's overland journey to the west in 1881, on both the outbound and homeward voyages.

In the meantime, Winnipeg having become a city of nearly eight thousand, the provincial government had sent a delegation to Ottawa to request a proper Government House. The request was readily acceded to by the Macdonald government, and plans were drawn up by the Public Works architect in Ottawa, Thomas Seaton Scott (1836-1895), designer of the West Block tower on Parliament Hill.

The site was on a tract of land beside the Assiniboine, which was already designated for government use, and which today accommodates both the Legislative Building and Government House. As the soil here was a particularly deep alluvial deposit, the house was made to stand on an "H" of rubble resting on oak piles driven into the ground. The style was the "Italianate" version of the fashionable Second Empire of the 1870s, "modified", in the architect's words, "to suit the requirements of the climate".[8] The walls were of the local buff brick trimmed with stone. A square tower rose above the roof line of the front facing Kennedy Street. The elevation shows a symmetrical arrangement of windows with segmented arches and a mansard roof with dormers. The massive wooden porch and the bay windows of rectangular design on each side wall gave the only hint of the Romanesque massiveness that characterized the metropolitan architecture of the 1880s.

On the interior of the ground floor the principal rooms were designed to connect with each other by means of folding doors, in order to give the illusion of greater space. On the north side of the house, off a central hall with its grand staircase, were a library (now the front drawing room) and a breakfast room (now the middle drawing room). Across the back, or west,

Government House, Winnipeg. Photograph by William Notman & Son, c.1884.

side were a large drawing room (now the back drawing room) and the dining room, both of which were given added importance by the bay windows already referred to. On the south, or river, side were the lieutenant governor's study (now the A.D.C.'s room) at the front, and a serving room with a lift from the basement behind it (now the cloak rooms). On the first floor were one large bedroom and sitting room and four other bedrooms, one bath and water closet, and a billiards room in the tower. The attics provided space for more bedrooms and a bath, and the basement for kitchen, scullery, pantry, wine cellar, stillroom, servants' hall and bath, and a furnace. The principal rooms, besides their steam radiators, were heated by

Government House, Winnipeg: the Front Drawing Room, looking into Middle and Back Drawing Rooms. From a half-tone, c.1904.

A Garden Party at Government House, Winnipeg, August 1899. Photograph by American Art Gallery, Winnipeg.

the tiled corner fireplaces so popular in this period. "Deafening boards" were placed between the floors against noise, inside shutters for extra protection from the cold, and electric bells to call the servants.

Contracts were let in 1881, construction by the federal government began in 1883, and the new lieutenant governor, James Aikins, moved from Fort Garry into the house in September of the latter year. The first two years, before the house was handed over to the province in 1885, saw certain improvements necessary or desirable for occupation, including drains, stables, wood shed, wash house, gardens, iron cresting on the roofs and a telephone.

Though some pieces of furniture were brought from Fort Garry, the furnishings were mostly new, purchased out of a fund of $15,000 allocated by the federal authorities. To judge from photographs published at the turn of the century, the furniture consisted of the fashionable items of the day: Rococo Revival chairs and sofas in walnut and mahogany, overstuffed armchairs, a large ottoman, stationary rocking chairs, elaborately carved sideboards and piano, and tables with heavily fringed covers. The walls were papered in emphatic floral patterns, the windows draped with lace curtains, the doorways festooned with *portières* and the floors covered with flowered carpet. From plaster flowers on the ceilings hung gasoliers, their luxuriantly curving branches supporting glass shades in a "delicate tint of yellow, which enhanced the beauty of the ladies".[9] The newspaper account of an "at home" held by Sir John and Lady Schultz conveys the period flavour of the house in late Victorian times:

> Upstairs the long supper room was a scene of brilliancy and splendour, the bright lights being reflected from the cut glass and silver. The table extended the whole length of the house, and was tastefully decorated with choice flowers, palms and tempting viands, while the constant

hum of merry voices and the delightful music swelling up from below made the whole scene one of perfect enchantment.[10]

During the terms of James Patterson (1895-1900) and Sir Daniel McMillan (1900-11) Manitoba enjoyed her share of the prosperity of the Laurier era, and Government House underwent a general overhaul in preparation for the visit of the Duke and Duchess of York in 1901. A ballroom was added to the north side of the house and a veranda to the east front. Much new furniture was bought, presumably the Chippendale reproduction chairs which are still in the house. The royal visitors spent only one day, but long enough, according to Sir Joseph Pope who accompanied them, to be given a "perfect luncheon" and in the evening a grand ball. Both functions were held in the new ballroom with its "myriad lights and superb floral display with mirrors".[11] A touch of lingering Victorianism was lent to the proceedings by a young lady who sang Tennyson's "Break, break, break, / On thy cold grey stones, O sea!"; another lady rendered "Dreams", and a gentleman "The Troubadour".

In 1908 the present vestibule replaced the porch, and a palm room and a new greenhouse were added at the end of the dining room, which now boasted an "Egyptian frieze"; and in 1911 the inventory of the contents of the house listed a collection of "stuffed heads". A few years later, when the huge new Legislative Building was being built in the imperial British version of the Beaux-Arts style, with a handsome reception room for the lieutenant governor, its architect Frank Worthington Simon proposed a grand Government House to match. But in the end the lieutenant governor had to be content with the old house, to which repairs were made in 1916. By the mid-twenties a garage had been built for the official car; but in the period of James McGregor, who held office during the depression, this housed only a Ford.

Government House, Winnipeg: Furniture of c.1883.

Visit of Lord and Lady Byng to Government House, Winnipeg, 1922. Front row beginning third from left: Lady Aikins; Lady Byng; Sir James Aikins, Lieutenant Governor; Lord Byng. Photograph by Foote.

The Duke of Devonshire's Visit to Government House, Winnipeg, February 1917. Front row: the Duke of Devonshire and his daughter Lady Maud Cavendish; back: members of the Governor General's Household including Lord Richard Nevill, right.

Whether or not it was into this Model "T" that his daughter eloped through a window with her young man is not known.

Punctuating the regular activities of an official residence came the visits of governors general. For Lord and Lady Aberdeen in 1894, Sir John and Lady Schultz held a State dinner and ball for a thousand guests. The two great tents and three dressing tents were abandoned when a storm burst, but space was somehow found in the house for dancing the Red River jig. Lady Aberdeen spent most of her time organizing yet another Local Council of Women. Three years later she found Lady Schultz opposed to her efforts and noted that Sir John was desperately trying to stay in office whilst the Liberals in Ottawa were pushing in Patterson as lieutenant governor as a "face saver" for his dismissal from the federal cabinet.[12]

When Lord and Lady Minto arrived in July 1900, on their way to the Yukon, there were Chinese lanterns in the grounds, and such an enthusiastic welcome for the Governor General (for the first time since he had stopped in Winnipeg as Lord Melgund on his way to the second Riel Rebellion) that his young A.D.C. Captain Harry Graham described Government House as "Liberty Hall". "His Honour Lieutenant Governor Patterson," he wrote, "has only one failing, and that is an appalling generosity, which causes him to give away anything that he possesses."[13]

Government House, Winnipeg: the Entrance Hall. Photograph 1982.

Government House, Winnipeg, with the new Assembly Room at right. Photograph 1982.

The Duke and Duchess of Connaught came in 1912, and the Devonshires and Byngs followed in 1917 and 1922 respectively.

At intervals before and after the First World War such assorted visitors as Winston Churchill, Stanley Baldwin, Sarah Bernhardt, John Philip Sousa, Amelita Galli-Curci, Ruth Draper, Sir Wilfred Grenfell and Laurens van der Post were received in the house. As elsewhere, the grandest of all visits was that of the first reigning sovereign, King George VI, with Queen Elizabeth in 1939 during William Tupper's term of office. From the Government House closest to the geographic centre of Canada the King gave a broadcast talk to the Empire. After the Second World War the Queen and Prince Philip, Princess Margaret, Prince Charles and Princess Anne have been among the royal visitors.

Government House, Winnipeg, is one of the few in the country to have enjoyed an uninterrupted period of use for its original purpose. The comfortable old house continues today, with an extension to the dining room and new assembly room, sunroom and green-house, to offer the traditional hospitality. Modernization has eliminated the corner fireplaces and folding doors. A fire-alarm system was installed, which for a time had a habit of sounding false signals at inconvenient moments during the visits of governors general and ambassadors. The occupants of the house have made their special contributions. Mrs Errick Willis, wife of the lieutenant governor from 1960 to 1965, recovered much of the old furniture from the attics and new furnishings have been added by their successors. Mrs Richard Bowles, in residence from 1965 to 1970, wrote the first and only history of the house.

Changing social conditions have been reflected in the size of the domestic staff over the years. In 1887 there were ten full-time servants living in. In the palmy days of the early part of the present century the number rose to fourteen but fell to seven in the 1940s;

Table laid for The Queen's Luncheon, Government House, Winnipeg, 1984.

Dr Yelena Bonner, His Honour George Johnson, Dr Andrei Sakharov, Mrs Johnson and Ms Janis Johnson in Government House, Winnipeg, 1989.

and today the work is done by considerably fewer. New conditions call for new methods, but Government House has remained, through good times and bad, as an example to others that change need not be an excuse for diminution of the dignity of the Crown. The activities of recent lieutenant governors have indeed only increased in energy and effectiveness and extended the influence of the lieutenant governor from the capital to the entire province. Under Mrs Pearl McGonigal and, since 1986, Dr George Johnson, the scope of the office has continued to broaden and to adapt to contemporary society.

Government House, Winnipeg: the Drawing Rooms, modernized.

H.M. The Queen in a chair first used by the Prince of Wales (Edward VII) in New Brunswick, 1860, with Pearl McGonigal and Mr McGonigal, in Government House, Winnipeg, 1984.

Lieutenant Governors of Manitoba

Sir Adams Archibald (1814-1892)	1870-1872
Alexander Morris (1826-1889)	1872-1876
Joseph-Édouard Cauchon (1816-1885)	1877-1882
James Cox Aikins (1823-1904)	1882-1888
Sir John Christian Schultz (1840-1896)	1888-1895
James Colebrook Patterson (1839-1929)	1895-1900
Sir Daniel Hunter McMillan (1846-1933)	1900-1911
Sir Douglas Colin Cameron (1854-1921)	1911-1916
Sir James Albert Manning Aikins (1851-1929)	1916-1926
Theodore Arthur Burrows (1857-1929)	1926-1929
James Duncan McGregor (1860-1935)	1929-1934
William Johnston Tupper (1862-1947)	1934-1940
Roland Fairbairn McWilliams (1874-1957)	1940-1953
John Stewart McDiarmid (1882-1965)	1953-1960
Errick French Willis (1896-1967)	1960-1965
Richard Spink Bowles (1912-	1965-1970
William John McKeag (1928-	1970-1976
Francis Laurence Jobin (1914-	1976-1981
Pearl (Kuhlman) McGonigal (1929–	1981-1986
George Johnson (1920–	1986

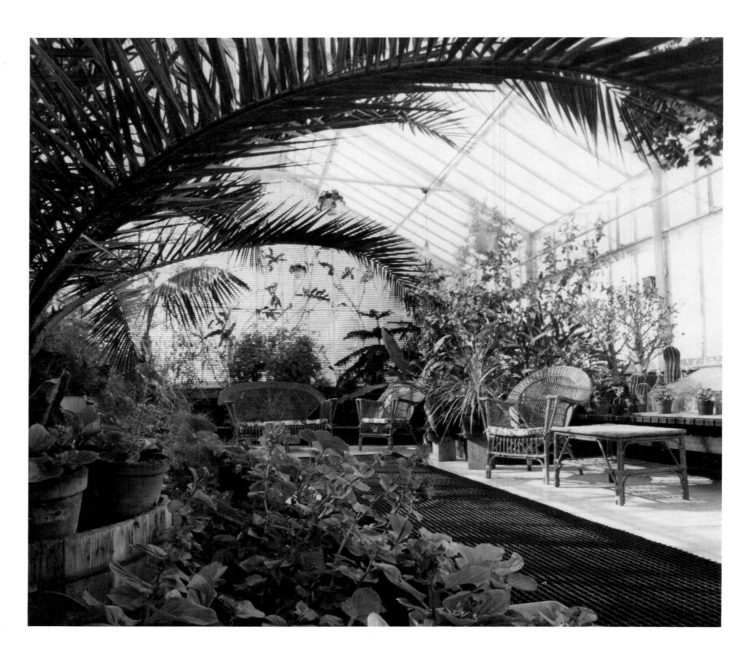

Government House, Regina: the Greenhouse restored. Photograph 1981.

The Northwest Territories and Saskatchewan

The territory which became Saskatchewan had, like Manitoba and Alberta, been traversed by early explorers and traders both French and English. The name had come from the great river of the prairies (Cree for "swift-flowing") and had been cited in its various spellings since the middle of the eighteenth century. After the Canadian government's purchase of Rupert's Land in 1869, and after the formation of Manitoba in 1870 and of British Columbia in 1871, the intervening expanse of prairie, woodland and arctic tundra became the Northwest Territories. In 1875 it was organized under a lieutenant governor[14] and council. The first shipment of grain from the prairie farms was made in 1876.

Provisional districts of Saskatchewan and Alberta were established in 1882, and in the same year Regina, formerly Wascana ("Pile of Bones"), became the headquarters of the North-West Mounted Police and capital of the entire Northwest Territories. Three years later the Métis, who had moved west from the Red River, rose once more against the Canadian authority which threatened their way of life. This second Riel Rebellion was quelled by General Middleton at Batoche, and Louis Riel was tried and executed at Regina. In 1888 the Territories gained an elected Assembly, and in 1897 responsible government.

With transportation provided by the Canadian Pacific, the southern parts of the Territory rapidly filled up with settlers from eastern Canada, the United States and the land-hungry nations of Europe. By 1905 settlement was far enough advanced to justify the formation of the new provinces of Saskatchewan and Alberta.

The first resident lieutenant governor of the Northwest Territories, appointed in 1876, was David Laird, a former federal cabinet minister from Prince Edward Island. Accompanied by his secretary Amédée Forget and a detachment of Mounted Police, he spent his first winter at Fort Livingstone on the Swan River near Fort Pelly. His "Government House" was a temporary wooden structure which had formerly been occupied by the commissioner of police. Along with living quarters it contained a chamber in which Laird held his first meeting of Council in March 1877. Later that year, after Battleford had been made capital of the Territories, he moved to this more strategic spot on the main trail to the west. By the time of the move a Government House was nearing completion at Battleford. A two-storeyed clapboarded log house, it was described at the time, and quite rightly, as the best house in the Territories. But it had little to recommend it except for a spacious reception room, which was put to good use by the Lairds and Forgets in entertaining the travellers and railway builders who passed along the trail. Dinner parties were lent local colour by the red uniforms of the police, and, as Forget was to remember, there were jolly skating parties during the long winters and carefree rides on the prairie in the summers. Here too Laird dealt with the problems of the period, especially the Indian unrest over the arrival of the settlers, and signed a treaty with the Blackfoot.

Life was not easy at Battleford for a family raised in the gentler climate of Prince Edward Island. Laird's wife and children departed for home in 1879. The Lieutenant Governor endured another winter or two before he too left the west in 1881. Forget stayed behind to serve the successor, the civil engineer and land speculator Edgar Dewdney, who arrived in 1882. It was Dewdney who pressed hard for the choice of Regina as capital of the Territories and was accused of doing so because of his investment in land along the route of the Canadian Pacific. Though in the end Regina was built a little to the east of his property, he succeeded in having both the Mounted Police depot and his official residence built on it.[15]

Thus the third Government House was situated on a ten-acre plot on the south side of what is now Dewdney Avenue in Regina. Tenders were called in 1882 for "the proposed house to be erected at Pile of Bones, N.W.T."[16] The result was a one-storeyed temporary building painted barn red, which was, in Sir John A. Macdonald's words, "made of portable frames carried from Ottawa and Montreal before the railway was built, and another portable wing has been added since":

> It is a wretched place, and I do not see how the Governor's family live there during the winter. I have occasion to know that their sufferings from the cold in winter are very great. There are 17 stoves going continually, and the inmates could not keep themselves warm. My wife was there during the winter, and although there was a stove in the room, the water froze.[17]

Government House, Battleford.

The First Government House, Regina, 1883: the Lieutenant Governor and Mrs Dewdney.

In spite of this the house was occupied for a total of nine years by Dewdney and his successor Joseph Royal. The latter was appreciated in Regina for his courtly grace, and outside the capital for his tours of the Territories, but less so by the Assembly for upholding the interests of the Indians and Métis. In Regina, perhaps to compensate for his troubles with the Members, he interested himself in building up the Legislative library. At Government House in 1889 he held a great ball, for which flowers were brought in from Manitoba. Later that year he welcomed the Governor General and his wife, Lord and Lady Stanley.

It was in Royal's period, with the railway bringing in not only population but an increased number of visitors, that a permanent Government House was agreed to by the federal authorities. This building, occupying a site just to the east of the old house, was designed in 1888 by the Public Works architect in Ottawa, Thomas Fuller (1822-1898), the versatile author of the Gothic Houses of Parliament and the Italianate Langevin Block in the federal capital. The style of the new house was also essentially Italianate; but considerations of economy in a period of recurring depression dictated the shearing away of nearly all ornament. The result was a long, spreading two-storeyed brick house which appeared to cling to the bald prairie as if for warmth. But for sheer size it was nothing less than palatial for its time and place. A recent socio-historical study interprets it as a conscious effort on the part of British-Canadian imperialists to counteract the American influence on the west.[18] This interpretation is somewhat of an exaggeration, to be tempered by reference to the old tradition in the Canadian provinces of providing a mansion worthy of the Crown as the apex of our constitution.

Government House, Regina: the
Central Hall. Photograph 1898.

Government House, Regina: the
Drawing Room. From a half-tone in
Saturday Night, 25 July 1914.

The exterior design was simple in the extreme. A sixty-four-foot main block, and a substantial service wing set back from it and extending it to the north, constituted the east, or principal, front. At the entrance was the arched *porte-cochère* which by now was *de rigueur* for Government Houses in Canada, and above this at roof level an acroterion bearing the royal cipher. This last, along with the little brackets under the eaves, the panelled balcony over the *porte-cochère* and the segmentally arched windows, constituted the only decoration. A skylight over the central hall was the only break in the continuous, low-pitched roof.

The interior was another matter. Fuller's plan of September 1888 — which was modified on the spot by an assistant, Maurice W. Sharon — provided a vestibule and a large central hall which rose as an atrium through the first floor to the skylight. All the rooms in the main block opened into this hall. On the ground floor, on the west side of the house, were the large drawing room and dining room, each with a shallow bay window. On the east front, to the left of the entrance, was the library, and to the right, a billiards room. On the south front was a small drawing room ("boudoir") adjoining the large drawing room. The wing contained

water-storage tanks and a hot-air furnace to supplement the heat given off by fireplaces in the various rooms.

Joseph Royal moved into the new house in November 1891. Within days the Regina newspaper published a glowing account of it:

> The Leader representative calling at Government House last week found His Honour busy at his desk but with his unfailing courtesy and "bon homie" ready for a chat. After a pleasant half hour spent in this way, Mr. Royal invited the visitor to inspect the new residence, and we gladly accepted the offer. A glance around the Governor's private library revealed a large roomy apartment plainly furnished but having every necessary convenience, His Honour's immense desk in the centre, and over the whole scene an unmistakable air of business. In fact but for the absence of clerks you might take the library for the office of a great railway manager.
>
> Stepping into the ante-room, or main hall, we found a spacious chamber, ornamental vases in each corner filled with century and other specimen plants from the conservatory. . . .
>
> Out of the antechamber are the entrances to all other parts of the building. His Honour first introduced us to the drawing room. This is magnificent in every respect. It is a double room, connected by an arch. The furniture is all on a splendid scale, but the pictures are what will most attract the visitor. All these are either steel engravings or kindred pictures — not a single bit of colour in the whole gallery. One elaborate steel engraving is exceptionally fine. It represents Her Majesty's Jubilee, and the ceremony in Westminster Abbey, with hundreds of celebrities portrayed with striking clearness, is admirably produced.
>
> Next we visited the dining-room, which is said, by those who know, to be superior to the dining-room at Rideau Hall. The walls here also are profusely adorned, chiefly with portraits of our leading political figures, living and dead. . . . Again entering the antechamber

kitchen, pantries, scullery, servants' hall, cold room, dairy and lavatory. Placing the domestic offices on the ground floor may be seen as an advance in convenience over the Government Houses in other provinces, where they were relegated to the basement.

On the first floor were six principal bedrooms, together with dressing rooms and baths, and the servants' quarters in the wing. In the basement were

Amédée Forget and his Secretary Frédéric Bourget in the Library, Government House, Regina.

we step into the billiard room, most conveniently fitted for the billiardists, the smokers, and the specta-tors. . . .

At His Honour's invitation we then donned our furs and walked down to the old house to see the conservatory* [where] there was . . . a lovely collec-tion of chrysanthemums . . . begonias, geraniums, fuchsias, heliotropes . . . coleus, abutilons, hibiscus, crown of thorns, century plants, oxalis, ferns, a great variety of bulbous plants and others in variety too extreme to particularize.[19]

This was evidently written before the building of the greenhouse attached to the house.

Royal's first guest was a French shareholder in the Canadian Pacific, the Duke of Blacas. The first dinner party, "at homes" and ladies' luncheons were held before Christmas, and a New Year's Eve ball which was reported in the press:

It was the universally expressed opinion among the guests of His Honour the Lieut.-Governor, and Madame Royal that the ball on Monday evening was one of the best, most pleasant and most brilliant balls ever given in the Territories. There was, in spite of the blizzard and almost impassable trails, a very large attendance, including nearly all the members of the Legislature, a number of visitors from outside towns,

and nearly all the fashion and beauty of Regina. The ladies' dresses were exceedingly nice — not "loud", but pretty — becoming, and in some cases magnificent.

The music of Professor Walker's orchestra began to float over the ball room at nine o'clock and there was soon a scene of gaiety and beauty that kept the eyes of the non-dancers rivetted. If the dancing and music were so bewitching, what shall we say of the refreshments and the supper? Needless to say, both were admirable, as in fact were all the arrangements. The courteous A.D.C., Inspector Drayner, was everywhere, infusing sociability into the company, and looking after everybody's comfort and pleasure.
On all sides were heard exclamations of admiration as to the convenience and elaborateness of the new Government House, which was splendidly arranged for the ball of Monday night. His Honour and Madame Royal were perfection as Host and Hostess.[20]

In the first few years of occupancy the house received such "improvements" as additional fireplaces and lavatories, which were doubtless needed by Royal's successor Charles Mackintosh, who had a bigger family. With his ideas of bringing civility to the west, this former Ottawa journalist entertained on a lavish scale and accordingly claimed an increase in his funds.[21] His pet project was the Regina Exhibition, the opening of which was attended by Lord and Lady Aberdeen in 1895. As ever, Lady Aberdeen was busy organizing a Local Council of Women in Regina, over which she met with opposition from the Women's Christian Temperance Union which she branded "American".[22] Over the mismanagement of the Exhibition, and a champagne dinner costing $800, Mackintosh brought down criticism on himself. His more popular successor Malcolm Cameron gave publicity to the Territories by entertaining a party of journalists from the United States. But he died in the very year of his appointment, 1898, before he had a chance to settle into the office.

Later in 1898 Amédée Forget, having served a long apprenticeship as secretary, came into his own as

Amédée Forget, his Wife and his Secretary in the Greenhouse, Government House, Regina.

The Maids at Government House, Regina. Photograph 1898.

Government House, Regina, decorated for the Visit of the Duke and Duchess of Cornwall and York. Photograph 1901.

lieutenant governor. So great was his success that he held the post longer than anyone who preceded or followed him. This intelligent and dignified friend of Sir Wilfrid Laurier and the Aberdeens was well placed to put his energy and vision to work for the Territories. He travelled far and wide through his wide domain. A man of many parts, he read not only the French authors but the poems of Walt Whitman. Not only did he make a garden in the grounds of Government House but planned for the future beauty of his capital. He was one of the first bicyclists in Regina. Of his wife, the charming but practical-minded Henriette Drolet, it was accurately predicted in 1898

that she would "make an ideal mistress of Government House. She is bright, clever, and an excellent conversationalist, and being of an exceedingly amicable disposition, is sure to preside with dignity and grace at the gubernatorial residence".[23] She was in fact to bring to the primitive Regina of her day high standards of housekeeping and an efficient household staff.

The early trickle of visitors to the house soon became a steady stream, as the importance of the prairies grew towards the turn of the century. Governors general regularly appeared on their railway tours of the country. Lord and Lady Minto paid their first visit in 1900, but their grandest came the following year when they were in attendance upon the Duke and Duchess of York.[24] After a drive from the railway station in Regina through "a sea of black gruel" which splashed their clothes, the Prince and Princess arrived at a house draped in bunting and hung with flags. They sat down to a State dinner which would have done credit to Rideau Hall:

Hors d'œuvre
Caviare sur croûte
Potage
Consommé impérial
Poisson
Poisson blanc, sauce tartare
Entrées
Petits poulets à la crème
Relevés
Filets de bœuf piqués à la Palestine
Légumes
Gibier
Caneton sauvage
Poulets de prairie
Salade
Salade russe
Entremets
Jubilee Pudding
Cheese pyramids
Desserts
Crème à la vanille, glacée
Fruits
Café noir[25]

It is said that the alcoholic editor of the Regina *Leader,* Nicholas Flood Davin, was so devastated at not having received an invitation to this dinner — though his wife had been asked to a reception — that he suffered a depression which led to his suicide the same year.[26]

The annual balls and New Year's levées held by the Forgets were the finest Regina had ever seen, and the number of guests entertained in the house amounted to

Lady Grey entering the Carriage for the Opening of the Legislature (Madame Forget in rear seat). Photograph 1905.

hundreds per year. The visitors' book[27] for the period reads like a Who's Who of the era. A mere sampling includes two future prime ministers, Robert L. Borden and R.B. Bennett; business magnates like Clifford Sifton and Sir Hugh Allan; journalists such as André Siegfried, who was collecting material for his book on Canada, and B.K. Sandwell of Toronto; the Ottawa city planner Nolan Cauchon; the poets Charles Mair and Pauline Johnson; the agricultural scientist Sir Charles Saunders, discoverer of Marquis wheat; the Toronto piano-builder Gerhard Heintzman; and the Montreal painter, Rita Mount, Madame Forget's niece. There were also visitors from Britain, France and other European countries and from the United States, New Zealand and South Africa.

At the formation of the province of Saskatchewan in 1905 Forget became its first lieutenant governor and held the post for another five years. At a luncheon on the inaugural day, 4 September 1905, which was

Mrs George William Brown in the Government House Landau. Photograph c.1913.

attended by the enthusiastic governor general, Lord Grey, and the prime minister Sir Wilfrid Laurier, a cable of congratulation was read from King Edward VII who at the time was taking the waters at Marienbad. An outdoor ceremony was graced by speeches by Grey, Laurier and the novelist Sir Gilbert Parker. It concluded in the evening with fireworks and a grand ball.[28]

An impression of lingering Victorian splendour is to be gained from contemporary photographs of the house and from an inventory of the contents made in 1906:[29]

> *In the hall:* three stuffed leather chairs, an oak settee, a hanging lamp, an Axminster carpet, a wall clock and four plaster statuettes by Philippe Hébert (of Sir John A. Macdonald, Sir George-Étienne Cartier, Sir Louis Lafontaine and Sir Hector Langevin).
> *In the drawing room:* a silk-covered davenport lounge, a sofa covered in bronze and blue damask, a cherry centre table, two other cherry tables, a mirror, rose-wood and oak chairs variously covered in yellow, red and blue, an angle chair, a piano and music stand, two bronze sconces with mirrors, a Wilton carpet, a Turkish rug, a cherry whatnot, satin and chenille curtains, china flower pots, a blue flower stand and flowered wallpaper.
> *In the small drawing room:* a plush-covered ebony settee, an oak armchair covered with blue satin and leather, a whatnot, a mirror, a cherry table, *jardinières* and yellow satin curtains.
> *In the library:* two leather davenports, a cherry roll-top desk, a flat-topped desk, oak book-cases, a revolving chair, a leather-covered easy chair with red and violet trimmings in raw silk.
> *In the dining room:* an oak extension table and eleven chairs, two armchairs, two oak sideboards with mirrors, three dinner-wagons, a velvet carpet and rep curtains.
> *In the billiards room:* a billiards-table, an oak sideboard, two "perforated" chairs, a wicker table, a cane-

> seated armchair, five oak chairs, a red plush settee, mounted elk horns and linoleum on the floor.
> *In the lieutenant governor's bedroom suite:* a double bedstead, a table, a bureau, an oak wardrobe, a writing table, a bed-lounge, an ebony dressing cabinet with mirror, a wash-stand, a stove and kettle and a metal bath sunk in the floor.

Later additions to the house included the greenhouse of 1901, attached on the south side, and the electric chandeliers of 1908 replacing the original gasoliers. In the grounds a collection of stables, carriage and sleigh houses, gardener's lodge, windmill, icehouse, henhouse and root cellar were all in place by 1906.

After the inauguration of the province the visitors came in ever increasing numbers. Lord Grey returned in 1909 to lay the cornerstone of the present Legislative Building; and there were the politicians including Mackenzie King and Borden; the Imperialists Lord Milner and Sir George Parkin, secretary of the Rhodes Trust; the poet and Indian agent Duncan Campbell

Visit of Lord and Lady Willingdon to Government House, Regina, c.1929. Front row, left to right: Edina Newlands, Lord and Lady Willingdon and the Hon. Henry Newlands, Lieutenant Governor.

The Royal Visit of 1939: State Dinner in the Ballroom, Government House, Regina.

Scott; the painter Edmund Morris; the Toronto concert pianist Mark Hambourg; and the industrial and railway great including James Dunn, Lord Strathcona, R.B. Angus, Lord Shaughnessy, Sir Edmund Walker and the young Vincent Massey. Organizations arrived *en masse*: in 1907 the National Council of Women, in 1908 the International Council of Women and in 1909 the British Association for the Advancement of Science.[30]

Such traffic in and out of the house, attesting to Saskatchewan's entry into the great world, called for further improvements. The grounds were fenced, the gardens extended and the staff increased (to include an

orderly from the Mounted Police at fifty cents a day). New furniture was bought, which seems to have included the reproduction Chippendale pieces that appear in period photographs of the drawing room and dining room. After 1907 responsibility for the house was in provincial hands.

Forget's long reign having come to an end in 1910, it fell to his successor George William Brown, who held office from 1910 to 1915, to receive the next royal visitors, the Duke and Duchess of Connaught. Brown was an enthusiastic early motorist, his wife a militant teetotaler. When she entertained the Women's Press

Club to lunch, with Nellie McClung as star guest, the appetizing summer menu of grapefruit, vermicelli soup, lobster salad, chicken aspic, lamp chops, meringues, ice cream and fruit gave no hint of refreshing drinks.

Brown's successor, Sir Richard Lake, held office during the latter part of the First World War. On one occasion he supported the war effort by addressing a Regina crowd from a tank. A year after the armistice he received the Prince of Wales, who did his official duty in town by visiting war veterans and military hospitals; but, as Lake recalled,

> His Royal Highness was very keen on exercise, and while at Government House got up every morning for a run before breakfast. . . . He was a most charming guest, and during his visit delighted everyone by his kind acts, thoughtfulness, and the interest he took in everything.[31]

The postwar period saw the occupancy of the house by the dignified Henry Newlands, a former Justice of the province's Supreme Court and a patron of music and theatre. In many respects his régime was the heyday of Government House. He received two governors general, Lord Byng and Lord Willingdon. Newlands and his energetic daughter Edina, who held a pilot's license, offered the hospitality of the house in support of many worthy causes. Their garden parties with tea tent and band attracted crowds of fifteen hundred. At one of Edina Newlands's teas, "The brightly lighted tea room presented a charming picture with its table covered with a lovely lace cloth — and a fire in the library".[32] In this period, stone gates were built in 1922 at the entrance to the grounds, and motorcars, a Studebaker followed by a Hudson, were provided by the government. The purchase of mahogany chairs and tables brought the interior of the house a little more up to date.

But the greatest change came in 1928 with the addition of a wing on the south end, containing a large

Archibald McNab, Lieutenant Governor of Saskatchewan, 1936-45.

185

ballroom with a separate entrance. Its interior was handsomely decorated in blue and gold. The wing also provided cloakrooms, a reception room and additional bedrooms upstairs. It displaced the greenhouse which was now relocated on the south side of the house.

The depression and drought of the 1930s had no immediate effect on Government House. Colonel Hugh Munroe, the lieutenant governor from 1931 to

Government House, Regina: the Central Hall restored. Photograph 1981.

1936, entertained the King and Queen of Siam and the governor general of the day, Lord Bessborough. But it was the self-made, ebullient Archibald McNab, appointed in 1936, who brightened up those dark years. Finding the official car "too showy", he preferred to drive himself about in his own green Ford coupé. In the summer of 1939 he appeared at the door of the house in his dressing gown to welcome the King and Queen to Government House. For the royal couple all possible splendours were arranged. The *porte-cochère* was decorated with large crowns and flower garlands. The State dinner in the ballroom, and McNab's parting words, "Come again and bring the kids", charmed the Queen who described the Lieutenant Governor as "one of the dearest old men I have ever met".[33]

McNab in his singular way attended more functions than any of his predecessors, was active in war work and generally kept up the dignity of his office by wearing the Windsor uniform at openings of the

Legislature and by holding new kinds of receptions such as the famous one for the cast of the Hollywood film "North-West Mounted Police" in which Madeleine Carroll starred. One of his largest affairs, and one of the last in the house, was his own golden wedding reception.

The victory at the polls in 1944 of the Cooperative Commonwealth Federation, the socialist party, heralded a speedy end to Government House. The following year the new premier, Tommy Douglas, declared the house "a frill, the relic of a byegone day",[34] and closed it down in order to save the $17,000 a year for its upkeep. The staff were dismissed and McNab, like his successors until recently, occupied a small suite of offices in the Hotel Saskatchewan. The contents of the house were sold at auction.

The subsequent history of the house has been one of thirty-five years in limbo followed by rebirth in different form. A large part of the grounds having been sold, it was leased from 1945 to 1956 to the federal government for use as a convalescent home for war veterans. In 1958 it became Saskatchewan House, a centre for continuous learning and, from 1964, the Regina Vocational Centre. For a time during the summers the ballroom was a theatre in which the re-enactment of the trial of Louis Riel was staged. In the prosperous seventies a revival of interest in the house as a monument of Saskatchewan history resulted in its restoration which was completed in September 1980.

The Government House of today has recaptured its original appearance. The rooms, painstakingly restored with period furniture duplicating that of 1891, are open for tours from schools and groups of the general public. The house and grounds are also used for official functions held by the lieutenant governor and the provincial government; and on 1 July 1984 the then lieutenant governor Frederick W. Johnson moved his offices to the old house. But this solution of

The Staff of Government House, Regina, before 1945. Left to right: Chuen, cook; Dewey, inside gardener; Marian Hinz, maid; Rupert, chauffeur. From the album of Irma (Laughton) Baker, upstairs maid.

Government House, Regina: the Drawing Room restored.

what to do with a repossessed Government House has not as yet included living quarters for the lieutenant governor, so that like the palaces of European republics, the house has the air of expecting its rightful occupants to return at any moment. Perhaps in the future a suite of rooms may be so arranged as to need little domestic help but yet serve as a fitting residence for the representative of the Crown in Saskatchewan.

Her Honour Sylvia Fedoruk.
Photograph 1988.

Frederick W. Johnson and
Mrs Johnson in the Greenhouse,
Government House, Regina.
Photograph 1984.

Lieutenant Governors of the Northwest Territories 1870-1905

Sir Adams George Achibald (1814-1892)	1870-1872
Alexander Morris (1826-1889)	1872-1876
David Laird (1833-1914)	1876-1881
Edgar Dewdney (1835-1916)	1882-1888
Joseph Royal (1837-1902)	1888-1893
Charles Herbert Mackintosh (1843-1931)	1893-1898
Malcolm Cameron (1832-1898)	1898
Amédée-Emmanuel Forget (1847-1923)	1898-1905

Lieutenant Governors of Saskatchewan 1905-

Amédée-Emmanuel Forget (1847-1923)	1905-1910
George William Brown (1860-1919)	1910-1915
Sir Richard Stuart Lake (1860-1950)	1915-1921
Henry William Newlands (1862-c.1942)	1921-1931
Hugh Edwin Munroe (1878-1947)	1931-1936
Archibald Peter McNab (1864-1945)	1936-1945
Thomas Miller (1876-1945)	1945
Reginald John Marsden Parker (1881-1948)	1945-1948
John Michael Uhrich (1877-1951)	1948-1951
William John Patterson (1886-	1951-1958
Frank Lindsay Bastedo (1886-	1958-1963
Robert Leith Hanbidge (1891-	1963-1970
Stephen Worobetz (1914-	1970-1976
George Porteous (1903-1977)	1976-1977
Cameron Irwin McIntosh (1926-	1978-1983
Frederick W. Johnson (1917–	1983-1988
Sylvia Fedoruk (1927–	1988

Government House (left), and Provincial Museum and Archives, Edmonton, c.1982.

Alberta

Having pressed further west than the explorers before him, Anthony Henday of the Hudson's Bay Company was in 1754 or 1755 probably the first white man to sight the Rocky Mountains from what is now Alberta. In 1793 Alexander Mackenzie of the North West Company crossed the territory by way of the Peace River on the first overland expedition to the Pacific. In 1795 the Hudson's Bay Company founded Fort Augustus, later named Fort Edmonton; and by the time of its absorption of the North West Company in 1821 the Company had a string of forts and trading posts in the region. John Palliser and Sir John Hector surveyed the southern part for the British government between 1857 and 1860. After Canada acquired the Company's lands in 1869, law and order were kept by the North-West Mounted Police, who founded Fort McLeod in 1874 and Fort Calgary in 1875. In the latter year the Canadian government organized the Northwest Territories. The first members from Edmonton and Calgary were elected to the Territorial Assembly in 1883 and 1884 respectively.

After completion of the Canadian Pacific Railway to Calgary in 1883, the ranchers and homesteaders began to arrive. In preparation for this the provisional district of Alberta had been formed the previous year; it had been named in honour of Princess Louise Caroline Alberta, wife of the governor general Lord Lorne and daughter of Queen Victoria.

Branch railways soon opened up the fertile tracts in the southern part of the district to settlers from eastern Canada, the United States, Britain and, in the early twentieth century, Scandinavia, Germany, the Ukraine and other parts of Europe. Two new transcontinental railways entered in the first decade of the new century, giving further access for northern wheat to the markets of Europe. So rapid was growth that by 1905,

The First Government House, Edmonton (1906-13). Photograph by Ernest Brown, 1908.

when the province of Alberta was created, it had a quarter of a million inhabitants. The first session of the Legislative Assembly was opened by Alberta's first lieutenant governor in 1906.

A dispute had arisen by this time between the two principal contenders for designation as capital of the province. The Alberta Act of 1905 had made Edmonton the provisional capital until such time as the matter could be decided. But it was settled out of court when the Liberal Member of Parliament for Edmonton and federal Minister of the Interior, Frank Oliver, advised the prime minister Sir Wilfrid Laurier to choose Edmonton. Calgary had little chance as its M.P. was a Conservative! In 1906 an act of the Legislature provided for an official residence of the lieutenant governor,

Government House, Edmonton.
Photograph by F. Rasch, 1914.

laid in coursed rubble work with limestone trim, the stonemasons having been brought from Scotland for the job. The style was a version of the fashionable "Elizabethan Vernacular," already adopted for the Government House of 1903 in Victoria. Two projecting gabled wings on the east front were joined at ground-floor level by a *porte-cochère*, the balustrades of which formed a balcony on the first floor. On the south side of the house was a columned veranda, also crowned with a balustrade, and a large bay window set near the back. The west side also had a bay window which extended up through the first floor, and which afforded a fine view over the river bank. A large greenhouse formed an addition to the back of the house.

The grounds, entered through iron gates in 102nd Avenue, were enclosed by spruce hedges and comprised a green park, flower garden and kitchen garden. In the grounds were also stables, garage and a green which was open to the Royal Lawn Bowling Club of Edmonton.

The lieutenant governor who inaugurated the house with a large reception in October 1913 was the first in the line of succession. George Bulyea was a New Brunswick schoolmaster who had become a member of the Northwest Territorial Assembly and commissioner of the Yukon Territory. A "safe and conservative" Liberal, he had a wife who was prominent in the Local Council of Women and in the Women's Christian Temperance Union. It is said that a ballroom in the house was vetoed by the Bulyeas because of their Methodist disapproval of dancing. Nevertheless they held an endless series of levées, garden parties, dinners and receptions for the Legislature and a variety of worthy organizations including the Victorian Order of Nurses, the Scouts and Guides and the Red Cross.

Particularly numerous among the signatures in the visitors' book[36] for the early years of Government

Government House Grounds, Edmonton, from the air. Photograph before 1967.

which would enhance the dignity of the province. In the meantime he occupied a good-sized Neo-Georgian house in Edmonton.

Government House, Edmonton,[35] was designed and built entirely by the provincial government. In 1910 a twenty-eight-acre site was acquired, high on the bank of the North Saskatchewan River, commanding a sweeping view of the country to the south. The land, which had originally belonged to Malcolm Grant, a pioneer of the area, had recently been sold to another party. An agreement was reached with the city of Edmonton whereby a bridge would be built over the Groat Ravine which lay between the site and the city. Plans were drawn up by the Public Works architect R.P. Blakey under the direction of the architect of the new Legislative Building, A.M. Jeffers. Construction began in 1911 and the house was ready for occupancy in October 1913.

The surface of this steel and concrete structure of three storeys and attic was clad with Calgary sandstone

Government House, Edmonton: the Reception Hall. Photograph by F. Rasch, 1915.

Government House, Edmonton: the Dining Room. Photograph by F. Rasch, 1915.

195

House were those of University of Alberta professors, headed by their indefatigable president, Henry Marshall Tory. They included, among the scientists and humane scholars he had recruited, the physicist Robert William Boyle, the petroleum geologist Ralph Leslie Rutherford, the endocrinologist James Bertram Collip, the classicist W.H. Alexander and the historian Alfred Leroy Burt. Each year's graduating class was also entertained at a special reception. Musicians and artists visiting Edmonton were regularly invited.

To all these functions the new house was admirably suited. Its interior, despite the Elizabethan exterior, resembled that of Chorley Park in Toronto in being eclectic in its decoration and furnishings. From the main door on the north front the visitor entered a vestibule giving on to cloakrooms on the right and the secretary's office and the lieutenant governor's study on the left. In the study, small *Art Nouveau* windows set into the doors gave a hint of the basic style of the interior: that of the Arts and Crafts movement, as at Victoria.

The large reception hall in the centre of the house also bore the marks of this latter style, in the very high wainscot of dark wood, the low arches over the doors leading into the other rooms, and the "Jacobean" stair. The room's most stunning feature, a square false skylight in the middle of the ceiling, with its emphatic rectangular divisions filled with leaded glass, gave a hint of the architect's familiarity with Frank Lloyd Wright's Japanese-inspired work of the period. Occupying the whole of the south side of the house were two large state rooms. The "blue" drawing room departed from the overall style of the interior by having an "Adam" ceiling, pilastered walls and elegant fireplace, all painted in light tones. A music room connected with the drawing room occupied a part of the east side. The dining room with its tiled fireplace reverted to the Arts and Crafts manner. Its dark wainscot was decorated with little strap-like brackets resembling those of Frank Lloyd Wright.

Government House, Edmonton: the Drawing Room. Photograph by F. Rasch, 1915.

Reception for Lord Strathcona,
Government House, Edmonton, 1915.

The first floor contained a billiards room, a Royal Suite, the lieutenant governor's bedroom and sitting room, and a series of guest chambers named the Rose, Blue and Green rooms. On the second floor were more guest rooms along with staff quarters and a sewing room. The basement accommodated the kitchen, scullery and other domestic offices as well as a steam-heating plant. One original feature, unique in Government Houses of the period, was a passenger lift to the upper floors, entered through a discreet doorway in the hall.

The furniture corresponded to the decoration of the individual rooms. As at Chorley Park it seems to have been mainly reproductions, though with some period pieces. The pantries likewise contained both everyday china and plated silver and best sets of

198   *Visit of the Duke and Duchess of Connaught to Government House, Edmonton, 1914. Beginning fourth from left: R.B. Bennett; ninth from left, Arthur Sifton, Premier of Alberta; Princess Patricia; H.V. Bulyea, Lieutenant Governor; Duchess of Connaught; Duke of Connaught; Mrs Sifton.*

Limoges porcelain and solid silver. A partial list of the furnishings is to be derived from contemporary photographs and the auction catalogue of 1942:[37]

> *In the reception hall:* a Jacobean centre table, settee and chairs; William and Mary oak chairs with cane backs, a stuffed sofa and easy chairs, a grandfather's clock, an Italian candlestick lamp, ormolu chandeliers and brackets, a Persian rug and flowered curtains.
> *In the drawing room:* Sheraton side tables, sofas and chairs covered in striped material, bow-fronted display cabinets, a mahogany display cabinet with Angelica Kauffmann medallions, a Chinese lacquer cabinet, an oval mirror, china lamps, glass chandeliers, Chinese and Delft vases, porcelain and bronze figures, a Sarouk carpet with oval pattern, silk tapestry curtains and a French screen.
>
> *In the dining room:* a table for twenty-four, and eighteen chairs with green leather seats, a bow-fronted sideboard with a pair of urn-shaped knife boxes, an Adam serving table, spider chandeliers and brackets,

William Egbert, Lieutenant Governor of Alberta, 1925-31, in the Study.

Government House, Edmonton: the
Dining Room dismantled, 1967.

Government House, Edmonton: the
former Drawing Room.

damask curtains and a Sarouk carpet with garlanded border.

In the library: a large desk, Chippendale chairs and table, and leather armchairs.

In the music room: a rosewood Steinway grand piano, a gramophone, a Georgian mirror, a chesterfield sofa, armchairs, a drop-leaf table, rose satin brocade curtains and a blue Sarouk rug.

The staff at the outset consisted of a housekeeper, cook, three maids and the grounds and greenhouse staff, with others hired as the occasion demanded. The daughter of John Campbell Bowen, the last lieutenant governor to live in the house, remembered hearing one of the gardeners rehearsing a tenor version of the treble solo in Mendelssohn's "O for the Wings of a Dove" as he went about his work; he was a member of the Cathedral choir in Edmonton.[38]

Important guests[39] including the successive governors general of Canada arrived in Edmonton as in other capitals. Another guest was Lord Strathcona, then in his eighties. Bulyea left office in 1915, and it was his successor Dr Robert George Brett, founder of the Banff Sanitarium, who received the Prince of Wales during the triumphal tour of 1919. The guests of various lieutenant governors over the year showed a great variety, among them Dinty Moore, creator of the comic strip "Maggie and Jiggs", the English actor Sir John Martin-Harvey, Field Marshal the Earl Haig, the Quebec premier Honoré Mercier, and the choir of His Majesty's Chapel of the Savoy. One of the last great affairs held in the grounds was a garden party for Lord and Lady Tweedsmuir in 1936, complete with marquee and tea tent.

Hardly ten years had passed since the opening of Government House when the Legislature, dominated by the United Farmers Party, voted to close it in order to save the cost of upkeep. But the vote was reversed, and instead it was refurbished in preparation for the visit of the Prince of Wales and Prince George in the year of the Diamond Jubilee of Confederation. In 1934, during the great depression, a resolution to dispense with the house (and even to abolish the post of lieutenant governor) was not acted upon. But in 1938 the Social Credit premier, William Aberhart, after his bitter confrontation with the federal government over unconstitutional money bills, took out his wrath on Bowen, who had been appointed by Mackenzie King, and abruptly closed the house. Consequently there was no place in which to accommodate King George VI and Queen Elizabeth when they stopped at Edmonton on their tour of 1939.

Government House stood empty until 1942, when it was leased to North West Air Lines for use as transient quarters for American pilots flying the Alaska-Russia supply line and engineers building the Alaska Highway. The contents were auctioned off and the greenhouse became a shower room for the men — with, one hopes, the glass whitewashed over for privacy. In 1944 the house was leased, and in 1951 sold, to the federal government as a home for disabled

Government House, Edmonton: the former Drawing Room. Photograph 1983.

Government House, Edmonton: the Central Hall. Photograph 1983.

Princess Margaret receiving a Gift from Peter Lougheed, Premier of Alberta, in Government House, Edmonton, 1980.

veterans of the Second World War. The rooms were by now in a sorry state. In 1964, in the grounds, which had been retained by the province, sites were found for the Provincial Archives and Museum.

A reversal of policy came after oil and gas had made Alberta affluent. In 1967 the province repossessed Government House and began to use it for official dinners and other functions such as the swearings-in of lieutenant governors and cabinet ministers. The transformation into the present conference centre was accomplished in 1976. The shallow back wing was extended to provide service access to the drawing room and dining room, which were now joined into one large room for receptions, dinners and meetings. The

His Honour Frank Lynch-Staunton in the Lieutenant Governor's Room, Legislative Building. Photograph 1984.

Residence of the Lieutenant Governor, Edmonton, from 1967.

other downstairs rooms were restored to something like their original appearance by the replacement of their moulded plasterwork and, in some cases, their furniture. The greenhouse was demolished. The two upper floors were made into a series of conference rooms of various sizes, including the large circular "Alberta Room" at the top of the house. In all these the decoration was modern.

Today Government House is used for many purposes including provincial, national and international meetings, Royal Commissions and the like. But vestiges of its original function remain in the lieutenant governor's levées, garden parties, receptions and din-

ners. At the house have been received the Queen and Prince Philip on several occasions, notably during the Commonwealth Games of 1978. Other members of the Royal Family, governors general and foreign heads of state (including Premier Aleksei Kosygin of the Soviet Union, who smoked the pipe of peace with the Indians in 1971) have paid their visits in recent years. Besides these, thousands of school children and members of the public have been conducted through the rooms.

For nearly forty years after 1938 the lieutenant governors of Alberta were obliged to live in hotel rooms. This situation was remedied in 1967 when the

204

*The View from Government House,
Edmonton. Photograph 1983.*

government provided the present "ranch-style" house in St George's Crescent, not far from Government House. It has been occupied by Ralph Steinhauer, a full Treaty Indian of the Cree tribe, Frank Lynch-Staunton and the present incumbent of the office, Helen Hunley. Too small for any large function, the new residence is nevertheless a comfortable modern house. Alberta thus illustrates one of the possible solutions to the problem of an official residence for the lieutenant governor in our day. Perhaps the future may see a return to the original idea of an august centre of provincial life.

*The Prince and Princess of Wales
acknowledging birthday greetings to
the Princess, on the balcony of
Government House, Edmonton, 1983.*

Diana, Princess of Wales at Government House, Edmonton, during the 1983 Royal Visit.

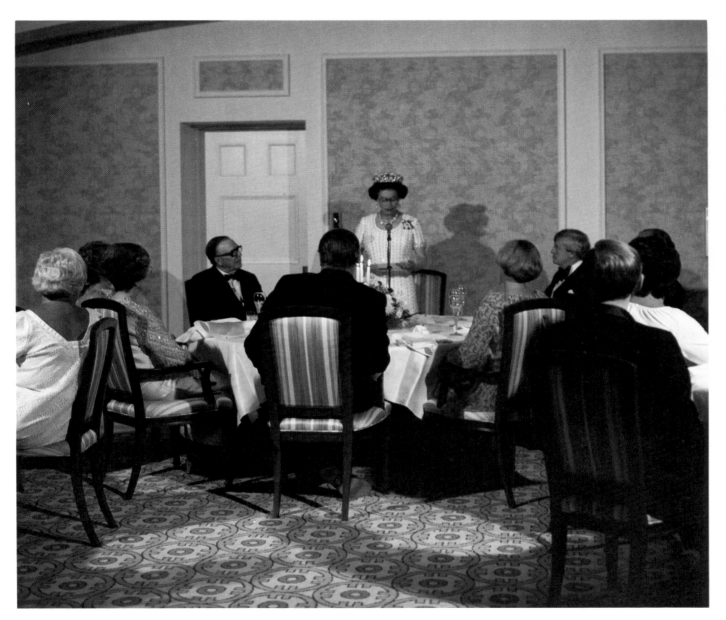

The Queen at a Dinner in her honour, Government House, Edmonton, August, 1978.

The Queen Mother with Her Honour Helen Hunley at Government House, Edmonton, July 1985.

Prince Charles delivers a speech at Government House, Edmonton, during the 1983 Royal Visit.

Lieutenant Governors of Alberta

George Hedley Vicars Bulyea (1859-1928)	1905-1915
Robert George Brett (1851-1929)	1915-1925
William Egbert (1857-1936)	1925-1931
William Legh Walsh (1857-1938)	1931-1936
Philip Carteret Hill Primrose (1865-1937)	1936-1937
John Campbell Bowen (1872-1957)	1937-1950
John James Bowlen (1876-1959)	1950-1959
John Percy Page (1887-	1959-1966
John Walker Grant MacEwen (1902-	1966-1974
Ralph Garvin Steinhauer (1905-	1974-1979
Frank C. Lynch-Staunton (1905-	1979-1985
W. Helen Hunley (1920-	1985

A P P E N D I X

Governors General of Canada from 1867

Sir Charles Stanley Monck,
4th Viscount Monck (1819–1894) — 1867–1868

Sir John Young, Bt, later 1st Baron
Lisgar (1807–1876) — 1868–1872

Frederick Temple Blackwood,
1st Earl of Dufferin, later Marquess
of Dufferin and Ava (1826–1892) — 1872–1878

John Douglas Sutherland Campbell,
Marquess of Lorne, later 9th Duke of
Argyll (1845–1914) — 1878–1883

Henry Charles Keith Petty-Fitzmaurice,
5th Marquess of Lansdowne
(1845–1927) — 1883–1888

Sir Frederick Arthur Stanley,
1st Baron Stanley of Preston, later 16th
Earl of Derby (1841–1908) — 1888–1893

John Campbell Gordon, 7th Earl of
Aberdeen, later Marquess of Aberdeen
and Temair (1847–1934) — 1893–1898

Gilbert John Elliot, 4th Earl of Minto
(1854–1914) — 1898–1904

Edward Albert, 4th Earl Grey
(1851–1917) — 1904–1911

Prince Arthur, Duke of Connaught
(1850–1942) — 1911–1916

Victor Christian William Cavendish, 9th
Duke of Devonshire (1868–1938) — 1916–1921

Julian Byng, 1st Baron Byng of Vimy,
later Viscount Byng (1862–1935) — 1921–1926

Freeman Freeman-Thomas,
1st Viscount Willingdon, later
Marquess (1866–1941) — 1926–1931

Vere Brabazon Ponsonby, 9th Earl of
Bessborough (1880–1956) — 1931–1935

John Buchan, 1st Baron Tweedsmuir
(1875–1940) — 1935–1940

Prince Alexander of Teck, later Earl of
Athlone (1874–1957) — 1940–1946

Sir Harold Alexander, 1st Viscount
Alexander of Tunis, later Earl
(1891–1969) — 1946–1952

Vincent Massey (1887–1967) — 1952–1959

Georges-Philias Vanier (1888–1967) — 1959–1967

Roland Michener (1900– — 1967–1974

Jules Léger (1913–1980) — 1974–1979

Edward Schreyer (1935– — 1979–1984

Jeanne Sauvé (1922– — 1984

N O T E S

Abbreviations

OA   Ontario Archives, Toronto
PAA   Public Archives of Alberta, Edmonton
PAC   Public Archives of Canada, Ottawa
PANB   Provincial Archives of New Brunswick, Fredericton
PANL   Provincial Archives of Newfoundland and Labrador, St John's
PANS   Public Archives of Nova Scotia, Halifax
PRO   Public Records Office, London
SAB   Saskatchewan Archives Board, Regina

Introduction

1. R.H. Hubbard, *Rideau Hall, an Illustrated History of Government House, Ottawa* (Montreal and London, 1977), p. 67.

2. John T. Saywell, *The Office of Lieutenant-Governor* (Toronto, 1957).

3. Jacques Monet, *The Canadian Crown* (Toronto and Vancouver, 1979), pp. 24-25.

4. Hubbard, *Rideau Hall*, op. cit.

5. R.H. Hubbard, "Ample Mansions, the Pre-Confederation Government Houses of the Provinces", *Transactions of the Royal Society of Canada,* 4th ser., XV, 1977, 263-285.

Part One: New France

1. See H.P. Biggar, ed., *The Works of Samuel de Champlain,* 6 vols. (Toronto, Champlain Society, 1922-1936), 1: 275-278, 310ff; Pl. opp. p. 278. See also W.F. Ganong, "Dochet (Ste. Croix) Island", *Transactions of the Royal Society of Canada,* 2nd ser., vol. 8, Section II, 1902-3, 127-231; and Ralph Smith, "St. Croix Island", *The Beaver,* No. 36 (Spring 1978): 36-40.

2. Champlain, *Works,* 1: 367-458, Pl. following p. 373.

3. For the successive residences at Quebec, see Ernest Gagnon, *Le fort et le château Saint-Louis (Québec), étude archéologique et*

historique (Montreal, 1895). The most comprehensive study is the lavishly illustrated Luc Noppen, Claude Paulette and Michael Tremblay, *Québec, trois siècles d'architecture* (Quebec, 1979).

4. Champlain, *Works,* 2: 39, Pl. opp. 39.

5. Translation by John Squair in Champlain, *Works,* 2: 35-36.

6. Noppen, *Québec,* p. 5, Figs. 4-7.

7. *Ibid.,* p. 5, Fig. 4.

8. *Ibid.,* p. 10, Fig. 13 and colour plate 4 (p. 102); p. 273, Figs. 2, 4.

9. *Ibid.,* p. 273, Fig. 3.

10. *Journal des Jésuites,* ed. by Laverdière and Casgrain (1874), p. 24, translated in Sir James Le Moine, *Picturesque Quebec* (Quebec, 1882), p. 24, note.

11. Gagnon, *Le fort et le château Saint-Louis,* pp. 35-36.

12. Pierre-Georges Roy, *La ville de Québec sous le régime français* (Quebec, 1930), 1: 535.

13. Noppen, *Québec,* p. 26 (Fig. 26), 274 (Fig. 7).

14. Claude-Charles de La Potherie, *L'histoire de l'Amérique septentrionale,* quoted in Roy, *Ville de Québec,* pp. 535-536; tr. by the author. This passage appears to have been written in anticipation of the additions to the building made in 1724.

15. Noppen, *Québec,* p. 254 (colour plate 22).

16. Luc Noppen and Marc Grignon, *L'art de l'architecture* (exhibition catalogue, Quebec, 1983), pp. 128-129, No. 8, Pl. iii. See also a drawing by William Morrison reproduced in Noppen, *Québec,* p. 274 (Fig. 8).

17. *Dictionary of Canadian Biography,* 3: 50.

18. Pehr Kalm, *The America of 1750: Peter Kalm's Travels in North America,* ed. Adolph B. Benson (New York, 1937), 2: 504-506.

19. *Ibid.,* pp. 427, 464-465.

20. Gagnon, *Le fort et le château Saint-Louis,* pp. 162-163.

21. *Ibid.,* p. 130.

22. See J.S. McLennan, *Louisbourg from its Foundation to its Fall, 1713-1758* (Sydney, N.S., 1957); "Contributions from the Fortress of Louisbourg", in *Canadian Historic Sites: Occasional Papers in Archeology and History,* No. 2 (1971), No. 3 (1978).

Part Two: Quebec & Lower Canada

1. John Knox, *An Historical Journal of the Campaign in North America*, ed. by Arthur G. Doughty (Toronto, Champlain Society, 1914-1916), 2: 204, note.

2. See Noppen, *Québec* p. 274 (Fig. 8).

3. Frances Brooke, *The History of Emily Montague* (1769; New Canadian Library ed., Toronto, 1961), pp. 172, 224.

4. Sir James Le Moine, *Picturesque Quebec* (Quebec, 1882), pp. 232-235.

5. Noppen, *Québec*, p. 275 (Figs. 9, 10); Christina Cameron and Jean Trudel, *Québec au temps de James Patterson Cockburn*, plates on pp. 95-99 (colour).

5a. Louise Hall Tharp, *The Baroness and the General* (Boston and Toronto, 1962), p. 366.

6. Philippe Aubert de Gaspé, *Mémoires* (Ottawa, 1866), p. 34.

7. Mary Quayle Innis, ed., *Mrs. Simcoe's Diary* (Toronto, 1965), p. 44.

8. Isaac Weld, *Travels through the States of North America and the Provinces of Upper and Lower Canada* (1799; London, 1800 ed.), p. 249.

9. Noppen, *Québec*, p. 275 (Figs. 9, 10); Cameron and Trudel, *Cockburn*, plates on pp. 95, 98, 99 and p. 92 (colour).

10. See Thomas Fowler's diary, quoted in Cameron and Trudel, *Cockburn*, p. 46.

11. Joseph Bouchette, *A Topographical Description of the Province of Lower Canada* (London, 1815), p. 432.

12. Aubert de Gaspé, *Mémoires*, p. 463.

13. *The Dalhousie Journals*, ed. by Marjorie Whitelaw, 3 vols. (Ottawa, 1978-82), 2: 25-26.

14. *Ibid.*, 1: 167-170; 3: 120, 142, 146, 156, 170.

15. Lady Aylmer, "Recollections of Canada", in *Rapport de l'Archiviste de la Province du Québec*, 1934-35 (Quebec, 1935), pp. 292-293.

16. Noppen, *Québec*, p. 278 (Fig. 15).

17. Charles Dickens, *American Notes* (1842; National ed., vol. 12, London, 1907), p. 245.

17a. Lord Monck Kerr, *Canada: on the staff of the Earl of Elgin, Governor-General* (privately printed, 1891), p. 5. This diary, covering 1847-9, is a spirited account of the period.

18. Dickens, *American Notes, op cit.*, pp. 245-246.

19. For the history of Spencer Wood/Bois de Coulonge, see Clément-T. Dussault, *Bois de Coulonge (Cahiers d'histoire*, No. 2, Quebec, 1950); Gérard Machelosse, "Bois de Coulonge, résidence de nos gouverneurs, et ses alentours" (*Cahiers des Dix*, No. 27, 1962), pp. 187-213; André Bernier, *Le vieux Sillery (Cahiers du Patrimoine*, Quebec, 1977), pp. 59-67.

20. From a letter to the daughter of Henry Atkinson, quoted in Lemoine, *Picturesque Quebec*, p. 337. For the architecture of Powell Place/Spencer Wood, see France Gagnon-Pratte, *L'architecture et la nature à Québec au dix-neuvième siècle: les villas* (Quebec, 1980); Noppen, *Québec*, p. 57 (Fig. 67).

21. Cameron and Trudel, *Cockburn*, p. 148.

22. Gagnon-Pratte, *L'architecture et la nature*, p. 25, (Fig. 28).

23. *Mrs. Simcoe's Diary*, p. 147.

24. Aubert de Gaspé, *Mémoires*; translated in Le Moine, *Picturesque Quebec*, pp. 343-344.

25. Le Moine, *Picturesque Quebec*, p. 346, note.

26. *Ibid.*, p. 336.

27. Quoted in Le Moine, *Picturesque Quebec*, pp. 336-337.

28. Quoted in Le Moine, *Picturesque Quebec*, pp. 332-333.

29. Noppen, *Québec*, p. 73 (Fig. 95); Gagnon-Pratte, *L'architecture et la nature*, p. 79; Noppen and Grignon, *L'art de l'architecture*, pp. 232-233, No. 72.

30. Donald Creighton, *John A. Macdonald, the Young Politician (Toronto, 1952), p. 187.*

31. Henry Arthur Bright, *Happy Country, This America: the Travel Diary of Henry Arthur Bright*, ed. by Anne Henry Ehrenpreis (Columbia, Ohio, 1978), pp. 336-338.

32. *Ibid.*, p. 344.

33. *Ibid.*, pp. 344-345.

34. Quoted in George M. Wrong, *The Earl of Elgin* (Toronto, 1906), p. 87.

35. For the Monck family's life at Spencer Wood, see W.L. Morton, ed., *Monck Letters and Journals, 1863-1868* (Carleton Library, Toronto and Montreal, 1970); Elisabeth Batt, *Monck, Governor General, 1861-1868* (Toronto, 1976).

36. Gagnon-Pratte, *L'architecture et la nature*, p. 125.

37. For the contents of Spencer Wood, see Archives Nationales du Québec, Inventaires de Spencer-Wood, made by the Ministère des Travaux publics, 1879-1925.

38. Batt, *Monck, Governor General*, p. 93.

39. R.H. Hubbard, *Rideau Hall, an Illustrated History of Government House, Ottawa* (Montreal and London, 1977), pp. 9 ff.

40. Noppen, *Québec*, p. 277 (Fig. 14).

41. J.T. Saywell, ed., *The Canadian journals of Lady Aberdeen, 1893-1898* (Toronto, 1960), p. 8.

42. Gagnon-Pratte, *L'architecture et la nature*, pp. 150-151.

Part Three: Atlantic Provinces

1. The one monograph on governors' residences in St John's is Fabian O'Dea, "Government House", in *Canadian Antiques Collector*, X, No. 2 (March-April 1975), pp. 48-51.

2. Quoted in A.M. Lysaght, *Joseph Banks in Newfoundland and Labrador* (Berkeley and Los Angeles, 1971) p. 146.

3. Paul O'Neill, *The Oldest City, the Story of St. John's, Newfoundland* (Erin, Ontario, 1975), 1: 137-138.

4. Some sources hold that Fort Townshend was not occupied by the governor until 1809.

5. PANL, Duckworth Papers. A reproduction of the drawing hangs in Government House, St John's.

6. PRO, Royal Engineers' Reports, 26 October 1825 (microfilm PANL).

6a. O'Neill, *The Oldest City*, 1: 140.

7. Quoted in O'Neill, *The Oldest City*, 1: 142.

8. PRO, Royal Engineers' Reports, 26 October 1825 (microfilm PANL).

9. Quoted in O'Dea, "Government House", p. 48. For Sir Alexander Cochrane, see Henry C. Wilkinson, *Bermuda from Sail to Steam* (London, 1973), 1: 338-339.

10. Quoted in O'Dea, "Government House", p. 49.

11. PRO, Royal Engineers' Reports, April 1827 (microfilm PANL).

12. *Ibid.*, 16 February 1831.

13. *Ibid.*, January 1827.

14. PRO, Royal Engineers' Correspondence, 1827-34 (microfilm PANL).

15. Author of *Newfoundland in 1842* (London, 1842).

16. O'Dea, "Government House", p. 50.

17. *Ibid.*, pp. 50-51; see also PRO, Royal Engineers' Reports, 1829 (microfilm PANL).

18. O'Neill, *The Oldest City*, 1: 149.

19. Robert Cellem, *Visit of His Royal Highness The Prince of Wales to the British North American Provinces and United States, in the Year 1860* (Toronto, 1861), p. 29.

20. *Ibid.*, p. 37.

21. 15 September 1860.

22. PANL, Inventory Volume by Alexander Harris, 1922, is a source of information on the changes made over the years.

22a. Nancy Grenville, "The Robbins are Singing very Prettily", *Newfoundland Quarterly*, LXXV: 1 (Spring 1979), pp. 20-25.

23. *Evening Herald*, St John's, quoted in O'Neill, *The Oldest City*, 1: 150.

24. Frank W. Graham, *"We Love Thee, Newfoundland"*, *Biography of Sir Cavendish Boyle* (St John's, 1979), pp. 170-173.

25. PANL, Government House Book of Dinners, 1913-1917.

26. O'Neill, *The Oldest City*, 1: 152.

27. Quoted in Charlotte Isabella Perkins, *The Romance of Annapolis Royal* (Annapolis Royal, 1952), pp. 12-13.

28. *Ibid.*,) p. 33.

29. J.S. Martell, "Government House", in *Bulletin of the Public Archives of Nova Scotia*, 1, No. 4 (1939), and J.S. Martell, *The Romance of Government House* (brochure, Halifax, 1939 and subsequent editions) are authoritative monographs; see also Sir Adams Archibald, "Government House" in *Collections of the Nova Scotia Historical Society*, 3 (1883): 197-208.

30. Quoted in Martell, "Government House", p. 2.

31. Reginald W. Jeffery, ed., *Dyott's Diary* (London, 1907), 1: 30.

32. *Ibid.*, 1: 36-37.

33. Wentworth to Duke of Portland, 25 April 1799, quoted in Martell, "Government House", p. 4.

34. C. Bruce Fergusson, "Isaac Hildrith", *Dalhousie Review*, 50, No. 4 (Winter 1970-71): 510-516; Robert F. Legget, "A Look at Another of the Unsung Pioneers of Canadian Engineering/ Architecture", *Canadian Consulting Engineer* (May 1975): 40-41.

35. See Martell, *Romance of Government House*, p. 10. The tradition is reinforced by a letter from an American architect, attributing the design to Robert Adam (PANS).

36. George Richardson, *A Series of Original Designs for Country Seats* (London, 1795), Plates LII and XX.

37. PANS, Sir John Summerson to John E.R. Devlin, 22 April 1975.

38. Martell, "Government House", pp. 8-9.

39. Brian C. Cuthbertson, *The Loyalist Governor: Biography of Sir John Wentworth* (Halifax, 1983), p. 110.

40. Quoted in Martell, "Government House", p. 2.

41. *Dyott's Diary*, p. 42.

42. It was moved to Tower Road and served as an Infants' Home until destroyed by fire in 1884.

43. Report to the Assembly, 30 March 1811, quoted in Martell, "Government House", pp. 15-17.

44. Thomas Chandler Haliburton, *The Old Judge; or, Life in a Colony*, 1849 (1860 ed., reprint by Tecumseh Press, Ottawa, 1978), pp. 72-90.

45. Herbert T. Silsbee, "A Secret Emissary from Down East", *Maine Historical Society Newsletter*, 2, No. 4 (Spring 1872): 107-125.

46. Quoted in Martell, *Romance of Government House*, p. 20.

47. PANS, Inventory of Property in Government House, July 1871. A total of $10,000 had been spent on decoration by 1864.

48. The original water colour is in the Royal Archives, Windsor Castle; the wood-engraving was published in *Illustrated London News* for 1 September 1860, p. 207.

49. Lady Dufferin, *My Canadian Journal* (New York, 1891), pp. 106-107.

50. Donald Creighton, *John A. Macdonald, the Old Chieftain* (Toronto, 1955), p. 255.

51. J.T. Saywell, ed., *The Canadian Journal of Lady Aberdeen, 1893-1898* (Toronto, Champlain Society, 1960), pp. 113, 415.

52. Quoted in Marjorie J. Thompson, "Domestic Life", in Frank Baird, ed., *Fredericton's 100 years, Then and Now* (Fredericton, 1948), p. 96.

53. PANB, Government House Commissioners' Records, 1820.

54. Southampton City Records Office, Smyth Letters, 1822-1824 (microfilm PANB).

55. PANB, Government House Commissioners' Records 20 June 1826.

56. PANB, Account of Repairs to the Late Government House, n.d., c.1826.

57. PANB, Government House Register, 1824-1829.

58. Mary Robinson, "The Old Government House, Fredericton, N.B.", *Canadian Magazine*, 27, No. 6 (October 1906): 491-498.

59. *Journal of the House of Assembly*, February 1826, p. 46.

60. PANB, Inventory of Government House, c.1895; *Catalogue of Government House Furniture to be Sold at Public Auction . . . Aug. 18th, 1897* (Fredericton, 1897).

61. See Charles H. Foss, *Cabinetmakers of the Eastern Seaboard* (Toronto, 1977), p. 44.

62. William T. Baird, *Seventy Years of New Brunswick Life* (Saint John, 1890), p. 108.

63. Now in the collection of PANB.

64. Lilian M. Maxwell, "The Royal Tour of 1860", *Maritime Advocate and Busy East* (July 1947), pp. 5-8, 29-30.

65. *My Canadian Journal*, p. 120.

66. *Canadian Journal of Lady Aberdeen*, p. 109.

67. *Daily Gleaner*, Fredericton, 20 August 1897, p. 2.

68. See Foss, *Cabinetmakers of the Eastern Seaboard*.

69. Quoted in Robinson, "The Old Government House", p. 498.

70. *Ibid.*, p. 498.

71. Mary Peck, "Report on 238 Waterloo Row" (typescript, 1974).

72. The sole monograph on Government House, Charlottetown, is the brochure, *Government House*, ed. by the Government House Committee of the Prince Edward Island Foundation (Charlottetown, 1971).

73. *Journal of the House of Assembly*, First Session, 1835.

74. *Government House*, [pp. 5-11].

75. *Journal of the House of Assembly*, First Session, 1835, Appendix C; included is an invoice totalling £561 from Bainbridge and Brown, Gray's Inn Road and Aldergate.

76. Quoted in *Government House*, [p. 2].

77. *Journal of the House of Assembly*, 1842, Appendix.

78. Cellem, *Visit of His Royal Highness*, p. 110.

79. 4 August 1860.

80. Quoted in Francis W. Bolger, ed., *Canada's Smallest Province: a History of Prince Edward Island* (Charlottetown, 1973), p. 149.

81. *My Canadian Journal*, pp. 101-103.

82. *Government House*, p. 3.

83. *Canadian Journal of Lady Aberdeen*, pp. 109, 427.

84. *Addresses to His Excellency Earl Grey . . . and his Speeches in Reply* (Ottawa, 1908), p. 161.

85. Chatsworth MSS, Diary of the 9th Duke of Devonshire, 2 December 1918 and 13 July 1920.

86. Heritage Trust, Charlottetown, Government House collections.

87. John Buchan, Lord Tweedsmuir, *Canadian Occasions* (Toronto, 1941), p. 29.

88. Quoted in Janet Adam Smith, *John Buchan* (London, 1965), p. 406.

Part Four: Upper Canada & Ontario

1. Lucy Booth Martyn, *The Face of Early Toronto* (Sutton West and Santa Barbara, 1982), p. 25.

2. *Mrs. Simcoe's Diary*, p. 170. Castle Frank was described in 1803 as going to ruin. It burnt down in 1829.

3. Eric Arthur, *Toronto, No Mean City* (Toronto, 1964), p. 15, Pl. 11.

3a. George Heriot, *Travels through the Canadas* (London, 1807), p. 138.

3b. John Beike to Miles Macdonnell, 19 March 1814, in Edith G. Firth, *The Town of York, 1793-1815* (Toronto, 1962), p. 329.

4. Marion McRae and Anthony Adamson, *The Ancestral Roof: Domestic Architecture of Upper Canada* (Toronto, 1963), pp. 112-113, Pl. 79; Arthur, *Toronto, No Mean City*, pp. 36-38, Pl. 30.

5. Hubbard, *Rideau Hall*, pp. 19-20.

6. Martyn, *Face of Early Toronto*, p. 98.

7. Anna Jameson, *Winter Studies and Summer Rambles in Canada* 1838), ed. by James J. Talman and Elsie McLeod Murray (Toronto, 1943), p. 46. It is to be noted that Bond Head was married.

8. Dated 1840; now in the Canadiana Gallery, Royal Ontario Museum, Toronto.

9. Dickens, *American Notes* (1842; National ed., 1907), p. 242.

10. Martyn, *Face of Early Toronto*, p. 67.

11. Donald Creighton, *John A. Macdonald, the Young Politician*, p. 223.

12. R.H. Hubbard, "Victorian Gothic", *Architectural Review*, 106 (August 1954): 108.

13. The best accounts of the Government House of 1868-70 are William Dendy, "Government House, Toronto, 1866-70", *Canadian Collector*, 11, No. 5 (September-October 1977): 21-25; and William Dendy, *Lost Toronto*, (Toronto, 1978), pp. 34-36.

14. Quoted in Dendy, "Government House, Toronto", p. 22.

15. OA, Estimate of Furniture for Government House, by Jacques & Hay, Toronto; OA, Inventory of Government House, February 1912.

16. OA, Records of the Office of the Public Works Architect, vol. 6.

17. Lady Dufferin, *My Canadian Journal*, passim.

18. Sir Joseph Pope, *The Tour of Their Royal Highnesses the Duke and Duchess of Cornwall and York through the Dominion of Canada* (Ottawa, 1903), pp. 109-120.

19. Quoted in Dendy, "Government House", pp. 24-25.

20. Quoted in OA, Hepburn Papers, Memorandum from Legislative Librarian to Premier, 1936.

21. Ontario. Sessional Papers, 1896, Appendix 2, Report of the Select Committee on the Maintenance of Government House in the Province of Ontario, pp. 183-258.

22. See OA, Hepburn Papers, Private Papers, 1936.

23. *Canadian Journal of Lady Aberdeen*, pp. 24, 441-442.

24. Dendy, *Lost Toronto*, pp. 176-179; Martyn, *Early Toronto*, p. 50.

25. Dendy, *Lost Toronto*, p. 177.

26. OA, Reports of Deputy Minister of Public Works, 1912-1917; Dendy, *Lost Toronto*, p. 177-179.

27. OA, Chorley Park Auction Sale, 1938.

28. See Herbert A. Bruce, *Varied Operations* (Toronto, 1958), pp. 223-227.

29. See Neil McKenty, *Mitch Hepburn* (Toronto, 1967), p. 139, note.

30. Quoted in McKenty, *Mitch Hepburn*, p. 139.

31. OA, Bruce Scrapbooks.

32. Fern Bayer and Judith Margles, "A New Look for Ontario's Vice-regal Suite", *Canadian Collector*, 15, No. 6 (November-December 1980): 45-46.

Part Five: British Columbia

1. The definitive study of the successive Government Houses in British Columbia is Peter Neive Cotton, *Vice Regal Mansions of British Columbia* (Vancouver, 1981). It is a model of its kind and I have relied heavily on it.

2. Douglas to Archibald Barclay, Secretary of HBC, 10 September 1850 and 16 April 1851, in Hartwell Bousfield, *Fort Victoria Letters* (Winnipeg, 1979), pp. 118-119, 172.

3. Quoted in Cotton, *Vice Regal Mansions*, p. 24.

4. *Colonist*, Victoria, 11 November 1864, quoted in Cotton, *Vice Regal Mansions*, p. 27.

5. Besides Cotton, *Vice Regal Mansions*, pp. 31-69, see Martin Segger, *Victoria, a Primer for Regional History in Architecture* (Victoria, 1979), pp. 277-279, 337.

6. *Daily Chronicle*, Victoria, 28 October 1865, quoted in Cotton, *Vice Regal Mansions*, p. 51.

7. Seymour to Duke of Buckingham and Chandos, Seymour Despatches, 10 December 1867, quoted in Cotton, *Vice Regal Mansions*, p. 53.

8. *My Canadian Journal*, pp. 273-279, 307-309.

9. Dufferin to Carnarvon, 8 October 1876, in C.W. de Kiewiet and F.H. Underhill, eds., *Dufferin-Carnarvon Correspondence, 1874-1878* (Toronto, Champlain Society, 1955), p. 270.

10. *My Canadian Journal*, pp. 307-308.

11. 27 April 1877, quoted in Cotton, *Vice Regal Mansions*, p. 62.

12. See Cotton, *Vice Regal Mansions*, p. 66.

13. W. Stewart MacNutt, *Days of Lorne, from the Private Papers of the Marquis of Lorne, 1878-1883* (Fredericton, 1955), pp. 112-118.

14. *Daily Times*, Victoria, 20 July 1952, quoted in Cotton, *Vice Regal Mansions*, p. 66.

15. Lansdowne to his mother, 11 October 1885, in Lord Newton, *Lord Lansdowne, a Biography* (London, 1929), p. 40.

16. *Canadian Journal of Lady Aberdeen*, p. 272.

17. Pope, *Tour of . . . the Duke and Duchess of Cornwall and York*, p. 98.

18. Rattenbury also speculated in land and manufacturing; he was murdered in England by his wife's lover. See Tony Reksten, *Rattenbury* (Victoria, 1978).

19. See Segger, *Victoria*, p. 277 *passim*.

20. Cotton, *Vice Regal Mansions*, pp. 75-76 and plates on pp. 83, 86, 88.

21. Chatsworth MSS, Diary of the 9th Duke of Devonshire, 20 November 1917.

Part Six: Prairie Provinces

1. The definitive monograph on the Government Houses in Winnipeg is Frances Bowles, "Manitoba's Government House", supplement to *Transactions of the Historical and Scientific Society of Manitoba*, ser. 3, No. 25, 1969-70 (subsequently published as a brochure).

2. W.L. Morton, *Manitoba, a History* (2nd ed., Toronto and Buffalo, 1967), p. 185.

3. *My Canadian Journal*, pp. 346-347.

4. John H. O'Donnell, *Manitoba as I Saw It* (1909), p. 71, quoted in Bowles, "Manitoba's Government House", pp. 32-33.

5. *My Canadian Journal*, p. 347.

6. *Ibid.*, pp. 349-350.

7. Morris to E.A. Meredith, 26 January 1875, quoted in Bowles, "Manitoba's Government House", p. 3.

8. Canada. Sessional Papers, 1882, quoted in Bowles, "Manitoba's Government House", p. 14.

9. *Free Press*, Winnipeg, 11 January 1884, quoted in Bowles, "Manitoba's Government House", p. 14.

10. *Ibid.*,

11. Pope, *Tour of . . . the Duke and Duchess of Cornwall and York*, pp. 71-73.

12. *Canadian Journal of Lady Aberdeen*, pp. 124, 252-255.

13. National Library of Scotland, Minto Papers, "Across Canada to the Klondyke" by Harry Graham (microfilm PAC).

14. Biographical material on the lieutenant governors is supplied by Donald S. Richan, "History of the Lieutenant Governors of Saskatchewan and the Northwest Territories" (typescript, 1980). Sources of information on their houses include A.R. Turner, "Historical Note on Government House, Regina" (typescript, 1958) and R.B. Shepard, "Symbol of Empire: Government House, Regina" (typescript, c.1980).

15. See Shepard, "Symbol of Empire", p. 5.

16. SAB, Lieutenant Governor Northwest Territories Papers, Tenders for Work at Government House, 1882.

17. Canada. Sessional Papers, 21 May 1888, quoted in Shepard, "Symbol of Empire", p. 6.

18. See Shepard, "Symbol of Empire".

19. *Leader,* Regina, 24 November 1891, p. 8.

20. *Ibid.,* 5 January 1892.

21. Shepard, "Symbol of Empire", pp. 12-13.

22. *Canadian Journal of Lady Aberdeen,* pp. 255-258.

23. *Tribune,* Winnipeg, 5 October 1898, quoted in Shepard, "Symbol of Empire", p. 13.

24. Pope, *Tour of . . . the Duke and Duchess of Cornwall and York,* pp. 75-76.

25. Government House collections, Regina.

26. Shepard, "Symbol of Empire", p. 14.

27. SAB, Government House Visitors' Book, 1898-1910.

28. SAB, Forget Papers, newspaper cuttings, 1905.

29. SAB, Inventory and Valuation of Goods at Government House, Regina, 1906; see also SAB, Public Works Records (Regina Office), Improvements of Government Buildings, 1895-1917.

30. Government House Visitors' Book.

31. Quoted in Turner, "Historical Note", p. 7.

32. Quoted in Richan, "History of the Lieutenant Governors".

33. Quoted in Richan, "History of the Lieutenant Governors".

34. SAB, Government House, newspaper cuttings.

35. Ruth Bowen, "Government House" (typescript, c.1976), Government House collections, Edmonton; this is a personal account by the daughter of a lieutenant governor.

36. PAA, Government House Visitors' Book, 1919-1930.

37. *Catalogue of Furniture and Fixtures of Government House, Edmonton . . . October 21st, 22nd and 23rd, 1942* (Edmonton, 1942).

38. Bowen, "Government House", p. 6.

39. Government House Visitors' Book.

LIST OF PLATES

The following abbreviations are used:

ANQ   Archives nationales du Québec
APS   Government of Alberta Photographic Services
CAG   Confederation Centre Art Gallery and Museum,
        Charlottetown
CP   Canadian Press
IBC   Inventaire des Biens culturels, Québec
MA   Manitoba Archives
NBHR   New Brunswick Department of Historical
        Resources
NFB   National Film Board
NGC   National Gallery of Canada
NSGS   Nova Scotia Government Services
OA   Ontario Archives
PAA   Public Archives of Alberta
PABC   Provincial Archives of British Columbia
PAC   Public Archives of Canada
PANB   Provincial Archives of New Brunswick
PANL   Provincial Archives of Newfoundland and
        Labrador
PANS   Public Archives of Nova Scotia
PAPEI   Public Archives of Prince Edward Island
PEIHF   Prince Edward Island Heritage Foundation
ROM   Royal Ontario Museum
SA   Saskatchewan Archives

Sources of illustrations are given in parentheses.

The Council Room, Château of Louisbourg, reconstructed (Parks Canada). *6*

After Théophile Hamel: Samuel de Champlain. Lithograph (PAC C-6643). *7*

After Samuel de Champlain: *Habitation de l'île Ste Croix.* Woodcut in the *Voyages* of 1613 (National Map Collection, PAC C-25617). *7*

Champlain's Habitation at Port-Royal, near Lower Granville, Nova Scotia, reconstructed 1939 (NFB; photo by J.F. Mailer). *8*

After Samuel de Champlain: *Abitasion du port royal.* Woodcut in the *Voyages* of 1613 (PAC C-7033). *9*

After Samuel de Champlain: *Abitation de Qvebecq.* Woodcut in the *Voyages* of 1613. *10*

Jean-Baptiste Louis Franquelin: The Château Saint-Louis, Quebec, of 1647-8, detail from *Carte du Fort St. Louis,* 1688. Dépôt des Fortifications des Colonies, Paris (IBC). *11*

After Charles de Fonville: View of Quebec with the Château Saint-Louis, *cartellino* in a map of c.1699. British Library, London (British Library). *13*

Gaspard Chaussegros de Léry: Plans and Elevations for the Château Saint-Louis, Quebec. Drawing, 1724. Archives nationales de France, Paris (Archives nationales de France). *14*

After Granicourt: Marquis de La Galissonière. Engraved by Hubert, 1780 (PAC C-31195). *15*

Anonymous: Le Bastion du Roy . . . Louisbourg (Archives du Comité technique du Génie, Paris). *17*

The Château of Louisbourg, reconstructed (Parks Canada). *17*

The Governor's Bedroom, Château of Louisbourg, reconstructed (Parks Canada). *19*

James Cockburn: *Chateau St. Louis, Quebec* (the Château Haldimand at right). Water colour, 26 June 1829. Royal Ontario Museum, Toronto (ROM 942.48.87). *22*

Anonymous: General James Murray, c.1770. National Portrait Gallery, London (National Portrait Gallery). *23*

Anonymous: Sir Guy Carleton, 1st Lord Dorchester, c.1780. The Earl of Malmesbury (NGC). *24*

James Cockburn: *Quebec—Place d'Armes* (the rear of the Château Haldimand at centre). Water colour, 1829. Royal Ontario Museum, Toronto (ROM 942.48.73). *24*

George Heriot: *Dance in the Chateau St. Louis.* Detail of a water colour, 1801 (PAC C-40). *26*

Anonymous: Project for the Courtyard Elevation of the Château Saint-Louis. Drawing, c.1808 (NFB). *27*

Sir John Watson Gordon: George Ramsay, 9th Earl of Dalhousie (NGC 7151). *28*

James Cockburn: *Chateau St. Louis, Quebec* (the Château Haldimand at left). Water colour, 26 June 1829. Royal Ontario Museum, Toronto (ROM 942-48-86). *28*

After Sir Thomas Lawrence: *The Earl of Durham.* Copy, 1908, of the portrait of 1829 (Rideau Hall). *29*

INDEX